RADICAL STATISTICS NUCLEAR DISARMAMENT GROUP

The Nuclear Numbers Game

Understanding the Statistics behind the bombs

Radical Statistics

This booklet was written by the Radical Statistics Nuclear Disarmament Group, which includes statisticians and social scientists, who are involved in teaching and research using statistics.

Contributors include:　Ben Armstrong
　　　　　　　　　　　Jeff Evans
　　　　　　　　　　　John Lintott
　　　　　　　　　　　Alison Macfarlane
　　　　　　　　　　　Ian Miles

We should like to thank the many people who provided early written contributions, made critical comments on earlier drafts, or helped with production, particularly typing; these include: Jill Adam, Mary Dean, Eric Eason, Martin Ferguson, Nicola Ford, Joel Gladstone, Wendy Goat, Valerie Gould, David Grimes, Andy Haines, David Jones, Mary Kaldor, Freddie Kater, Andrew Kelly, Bill Lavender, Carol Lee, Craig McFarlane, Gordon McKerron, Andrew Morris, Charlotte Morris, Barbara Pearse, Julian Perry Robinson, Paul Rogers, Martin H Ryle, Chris Smith, Dan Smith, Ron Smith, Philip Steadman, Steve Thomas, Anthony Tucker, and members of Brighton CND and St Albans Nuclear Disarmament Campaign (STAND).

Cover designed by Brian Lunt
Diagrams by Jane Macauley

We invite readers to send comments and corrections in response to this booklet.

ISBN 0 906081 04 1✓
Published by Radical Statistics c/o BSSRS, 9 Poland Street, London W1V 3DG.
Typeset by: Range Left Photosetters (TU) (01) 251 3959
Printed by Blackrose Press (01) 251 3043
Trade distribution by:
　Southern Distribution, Albion Yard, 17 Balfe Street, London N1 (01) 837 1460
　Scottish and Northern Books, Fourth Floor, 18 Granby Row, Manchester M1 3GE
　(061) 228 3903, and 48a Hamilton Place, Edinburgh EH3 5AX (031) 225 4950.

CONTENTS

FIGURES

INTRODUCTION

Anyone who is at all in touch with the problems of today's world will know that nuclear weapons are enormously powerful devices, that nuclear war would be a nightmare beyond description, and that military expenditure diverts vast amounts of resources from more useful production. Yet the so called 'advanced' countries of the world are busily engaging themselves in a new arms race. To seek public support for this, their leaders make pronouncements which sound plausible at first, but which require closer examination.

Statistics are often used to justify the need for greater numbers and new types of weapons. The media bombard us with statements that "we" need more weapons because "the other side" have superiority over us. For example, statistics are used to support the claim that the USSR's nuclear capacity in Europe is very much greater than NATO's. In addition statistics are sometimes used to make assertions about other countries' intentions rather than to describe the balance of terror itself. For example, the Soviet Union is said to devote a vast proportion of its economic resources to the military, while 'our' expenditure is small in comparison.

These arguments are aimed to persuade us that, even if nuclear weapons are undesirable – indeed, are manifestly immoral – more of them are needed to produce a plausible deterrent. Suggestions are also made that the effects of nuclear war have been exaggerated, and large areas of Britain would, apparently, be unaffected. Many people are, it is supposed, likely to survive, and civil defence precautions of the most rudimentary kind could increase this number dramatically. Mere wishful thinking? How can it be when statistics can be presented to support the case? One aim of this pamphlet is to show how it is that statistics can be used to allow us to think about the unthinkable and to justify the unjustifiable.

There are two very common views about the nature of statistics. One is that they are objective or neutral facts and the other that they are 'damned lies' plucked conveniently out of the blue to support whatever views are being put forward.

While we suspect that on occasion the latter may well be true of at least some of the statistics used in the debate about nuclear arms, in general it is a gross oversimplification which hinders a critical appraisal of many statistics.

Instead, we believe that statistics reflect the processes by which they are collected and the views of those who produce them. This includes the way in which they conceive of and define what is being measured, and involves their assumptions about its importance relative to the things which are not being measured as well as their wider views about the state of the world.[1 2] Thus, for example, the standard comparison of the numbers of tanks which NATO and the Warsaw Pact deploy in Europe assumes among other things that:

(i) The methods of counting them for the Warsaw Pact (e.g: counting tank sheds from the air) give results comparable to those used to count NATO tanks.

(ii) Both sides have tanks of the same age and capability, or if differences exist, they are irrelevant to the purposes of the comparison being made.

(iii) It is meaningful to compare numbers of tanks, without taking into account, for example, armoured cars and anti-tank weapons.

(iv) Both sides share a comparable notion of what a "tank" is, within their overall strategy.

In writing this pamphlet, we aim to point out some of the main ways in which statistics are used on behalf of the war drive, and to provide both material and critical tools for understanding and dealing with these arguments. These critical tools can also be used to help people decide when and how to use, attack, or reject data. Finally, we provide data on a wide range of background issues about which it is useful to be well informed, with references to fuller sources elsewhere.

The first section of this pamphlet takes on the thorny question of the balance of terror between East and West. The final conclusion about this precarious "balance" would depend on access to secret data and upon a host of assumptions concerning military strategy. Even without this though, it is possible to see that official dogma concerning the arms race rests on a very dubious basis and we outline an alternative appraisal.

The second section considers global issues of nuclear proliferation and the arms trade as well as Britain's military role in and out of NATO. We attempt to chart some of the social and economic costs of current military strategy and indicate who is most likely to benefit from it. The third section outlines the likely effects of nuclear war; while critical of the available data, it also suggests how they can be used to transform bald general statements about the consequences of nuclear explosions into illustrations relevant to local communities.

The final section gathers together some conclusions while also presenting some data about alternatives to nuclear war and the arms race. While it is hard to describe in detail alternative policies to those currently in force, we here present some data bearing on disarmament, conversion of military industries and non-nuclear defence strategies. This is followed by an Appendix which contains a brief guide to sources on both the data provided and further data.

The bibliographies for each section and the list of recent publications about nuclear war and disarmament point the way to the arguments which go beyond statistics.[3] For we would not wish to give the impression that all the issues that arise for peace movements can be expressed in statistics, many important questions cannot be discussed in quantitative terms. Furthermore, many issues which in principle might be illuminated by statistics remain obscure in practice, because of secrecy or limitations in the data.

Yet we have argued that the escalation of the arms race, and in particular the increasing production and deployment of nuclear weapons, are utterly without moral justification – and hence rely for their support on arguments about balances of force, comparisons of provision, likely intentions and probable consequences. Appeals to statistics are, inevitably an essential component of such arguments – as well as an essential tool in combatting them.

Because we are people whose work involves the use and interpretation of statistics we felt that a contribution which we could make to the overall effort was to help others to understand how statistics can be used to justify the possession and acquisition of nuclear weapons, and how they can be used to oppose them. We hope that this pamphlet will go some way to achieving that end.

References

1.   Irvine J, Miles I, Evans J. *Demystifying Social Statistics*. London: Pluto Press 1979.
2.   Radical Statistics Health Group. *The Unofficial Gude to Official Health Statistics*. London: Radical Statistics 1980.
3.   For a lucid presentation of these arguments, see Ryle M. *The Politics of Nuclear Disarmament*. London: Pluto Press 1981

1. IN THE BALANCE? THE STATISTICS OF EAST-WEST RIVALRY

1.1 INTRODUCTION

The case for Britain's nuclear weapons and its policy of increasing military spending is made in terms of the major international conflicts. It is in particular in the context of a possible war between the two superpowers, the USA and the USSR, and their allies that such a case is generally argued. In this chapter we therefore look at the information available about the relative military strengths of the two superpower blocks – The North Atlantic Treaty organisation (NATO) and the Warsaw Pact (WP).

Governments have privileged access to data on many matters, but in the case of military statistics this often amounts to a complete monopoly of information. This monopoly may be used to present a highly misleading picture with little fear of informed criticism.

We are sometimes able to spot discrepancies in the statistics which are presented. For instance, the estimate of military expenditure which the Government uses to show the rest of NATO that the UK is "pulling its weight" is higher than that used in domestic debates on the budget.[1] Information also sometimes comes to light when bureaucrats within the military establishment become disenchanted. For example Alan Enthoven, who was a US Assistant Secretary of Defence in the 1960s, became horrified by the way the Pentagon presented information and denounced it publicly.[2] Although he proposed more realistic assessments, the practices he denounced are still used.

We can, however, learn most from being careful to see government military statistics in the context of government policies and the whole "balance of terror" ideology. By looking at where the data come from and how they are produced in this light, we can get a fair idea of where the biases are likely to be and what conclusions, if any, we can draw from the figures. We cannot really expect to prove or disprove the correctness of any particular statistic, but we can equip ourselves better to deal with the overall arguments.

1.2 BACKGROUND

1.2.1 The Cold War

Starting in the 1950s, States with nuclear weapons claimed that they were only 'deterrents'. It was argued that the best, or perhaps the only way one major power would ward off an attack from another was to build up a large arsenal of nuclear weapons. The rationale for this was not so much to use the weapons, but to offer a *plausible* threat that they would be used if the country was attacked. This strategy was later given the name "mutually assured destruction". If one side attacked the other it would be inviting its own as well as its enemy's destruction. United States defence doctrine, outlined by McNamara when US Secretary of State, was based on the assumption that the ability to destroy between one third and two third's of the enemy's industry and between a quarter and a third of its population would meet this requirement.[3]

The MAD doctrine was used to justify the development of more sophisticated nuclear weapons, to ensure that warheads could be delivered through any conceivable defence. Initial reliance on free falling bombs delivered by aircraft was replaced by both superpowers by the "strategic triad" of delivery systems; aircraft, Inter-Continental Ballistic Missiles (ICBMs), and Submarine Launched Ballistic Missiles (SLBMs). In addition, short range "tactical" nuclear weapons were developed and deployed, first by NATO and then by the WP.

1.2.2 Detente

With the Detente policy of the late 60s and 70s involving the development of trade between NATO and WP countries and the beginning of negotiations to limit the arms race, a relative stability in the balance of terror seemed to have been assured. Government statements admitted that the nuclear arsenals already built up were easily capable of threatening MAD, and any further build up would be wasteful and was capable of being limited by treaty. The other side's intentions were portrayed as less aggressive than previously, and military expenditure (on weapons designed for world war not on those designed for more limited conflicts) grew more slowly.

1.2.3 The Present

Over the last few years the official view of the military situation in NATO countries has altered radically. Without denying that NATO have more than enough weapons to obliterate the cities of the WP countries, it is nevertheless argued that more weapons, and great increases in military spending, are necessary. This argument is based on two claims. Firstly it is claimed that it is necessary to be able to respond to an attack at exactly the level at which it comes ("flexible response"), rather than rely on the threat of MAD. Secondly, it is claimed that NATO is militarily inferior to the WP at certain levels of the "flexible response spectrum". Various "scenarios" (imaginary situations of East-West conflict) are presented to suggest areas of Western inferiority.

The first claim is a strategic doctrine followed explicitly by NATO since 1967. The assumptions behind this doctrine are contested by many[4][5] but since this debate does not have a big statistical aspect, we will not enter into it here. The justifications offered for the second claim of military imbalance often rely heavily on statistics. Without necessarily accepting the first claim, in order to assess the validity of the second claim we shall examine the statistics of the military balance in conventional as well as nuclear armed strength.

1.2.4 The Context of Military Statistics

We will look at the available statistics relating to military spending, size of armed forces, conventional arms, and nuclear arms. Before looking at the figures, however, let us summarise their context. NATO governments, for whatever reason, now wish to produce and deploy more nuclear weapons, and to spend more money on the military generally. Moreover they have to do this in a time of austerity. Now, as in the cold war, governments have every reason to exaggerate the enemy's strength and minimise "ours", and this is one tendency we can expect to see reflected in the figures. In addition, the shift in policy from detente makes it convenient to emphasize figures apparently showing that NATO's military inferiority is a recent development. Thus for statistics from NATO countries we should be on our guard against distortions in these directions. Since most statistics about the WP military come from Western intelligence sources, they are even more sensitive to the pressures outlined above.

1.3   THE BALANCE OF MILITARY EXPENDITURE

We begin with the type of data which in fact says least about the real balance of military power between NATO and the WP. It is also the type of data that is easiest to manipulate and most often is manipulated. Military expenditure is at best a measure of the resources devoted to military capability, and not a measure of military capability itself.

The data in figure 1.1 show estimates of NATO and WP military expenditure in the 1970s. Such data are often used to summarise the military balance, since by expressing the various aspects of the balance in terms of money they avoid the need for separate comparisons of personnel, warheads, ships, etc. There are a number of reasons why such a comparison is misleading. Furthermore the range of estimates which result can be used selectively by governments at their convenience.

Firstly there are problems of definition:–
(i) What items are included under the heading of "military" or "defence" expenditure?
(ii) Are they the same for all countries?
(iii) Are they all relevant to a conflict between NATO and WP countries?

Given the secrecy that surrounds military budgets items of military spending may be hidden under other headings and do not find their way into the statistics. On the other hand, items are included in "defence expenditure" which bear no relation to the capacity to directly fight the other superpower block. Other aims of military expenditure might include the wish to absorb unemployment, to police internal conflicts, or to fight wars not directly related to a NATO-WP conflict. Thus for example US military spending was very high during the Vietnam war, but this did not reflect a greater capability for war with the WP. The USSR devotes considerable resources to military preparedness against China. These factors vary from country to country making comparisons difficult. These problems are accentuated by different costs for the same equipment or personnel. More advanced technology can make the same capability cheaper. Higher salaries may need to be paid to a professional army than a conscript one.

There are serious problems in ensuring that the prices and exchange rates used make comparisons valid, especially since the way that prices are used in NATO and WP countries is quite different. The price attached to Soviet armaments may not reflect the "market" costs of production to the enterprise producing them, but may be decided on a different basis by Soviet planners. Thus Western analysts must estimate costs of production by indirect means. This inevitably leaves a wide margin of error, so that WP military spending can easily be exaggerated or minimised. In recent years the CIA, source for most published figures on WP military spending, has changed its basis for estimation. The new estimates come out about 20% higher than the previous estimates. This change does not reflect any increase in the actual military hardware and personnel that the WP has acquired, but as rather a reassessment of the cost of those resources. With the new way of estimating WP military expenditure, the sum of money estimated is that which would be required to purchase, in the USA, troops and weapons comparable to those of the WP. Thus if the US army gets a pay rise, the CIA's estimate of WP spending goes up.

Figure 1.1 NATO and WP Military Expenditure.[1]

	$ billion, current price				Current prices as % of GNP			$ billion, 1978 prices and exchange rates			
	1972	1975	1979	1980	1972	1975	1979	1972	1975	1979	1980
WP	90.4	131.9	na	na	9.5	9.6–11.1		104.4	110.4	117.6	119.6
USSR	84.4	124.4	na	na	10.8	11–13		95.4	99.8	105.7	107.3
NATO	113.2	149.5	202.3	240.4	5.3	4.9	4.2	191.1	185.5	191.8	193.9
USA	77.6	89.0	114.5	142.7	6.7	5.9	5.2	121.1	110.2	109.9	111.2
UK	7.9	11.1	17.5	24.4	5.2	4.9	4.9	14.4	14.5	15.3	16.2

1. NATO data include France but exclude assistance to West Berlin.
Sources: For expenditure at current prices and as % of GNP, *The Military Balance* (IISS)
For expenditure at constant prices, *SIPRI Yearbook*.

The use of one currency, often dollars, creates further problems, since official exchange rates do not reflect purchasing power. Using more "realistic" exchange rates opens up further variation in estimates, with further opportunities for presenting only "convenient" figures.

According to the Stockholm International Peace Research Institute (SIPRI), estimates by the CIA suggest that Soviet military expenditure is some 50% higher than US expenditure, while Soviet figures converted into dollars at the official rate suggest a Soviet expenditure of between a fifth and a sixth of US expenditure. SIPRI itself opts for estimates showing rough parity.[7]

These difficulties are compounded when we consider figures, not for the absolute cost of the military, but for the proportion of Gross National Product (GNP) devoted to the military. Given the much lower average GNP of the WP countries, their military spending as a proportion of the GNP appears much higher in comparison with NATO countries than does their absolute military spending. This does not mean that they are putting more resources into arms. In addition similar factors operate in calculating GNP as in military expenditure. The Soviet method is quite different (certain items which are included in the West are excluded, for example), and estimating Soviet GNP as it would be defined in the West adds to the uncertainty and to the possibilities for distortion.

The result of these uncertainties is that a wide variety of figures is available, none of which can be said to express "true" military expenditure, let alone the capability that such expenditure buys. Governments and media can choose from among these statistics according to the impression that they want to convey. For example, in the West we are often told that

(i) Military expenditure of the USSR is higher than that of the US, rather than that NATO spends more than the WP.

(ii) WP countries spend a higher proportion of their GNP on the military than NATO countries, but not that WP countries have lower GNPs.

(iii) The proportion of the GNP of Warsaw Pact countries which is devoted to military expenditure is increasing, but not that the apparent increase results from changes in methods of estimating WP expenditure.

(iv) The proportion of the GNP of NATO countries which is devoted to military expenditure has remained fairly constant over time, but not that the GNP has risen and thus military expenditure has increased also.

1.4 THE BALANCE OF MILITARY PERSONNEL

At first sight it would appear that there are fewer problems in using statistics of military personnel than in using expenditure data. They measure a specific component of the capability to wage war, rather than simply the costs this capability entails.

Once again, however, we are faced with the problem of what should be included. Some civilians may perform military functions and vice versa, and the way the functions are divided can differ from country to country.

One figure given by the Pentagon for the USSR's military personnel for 1976 was 4 800 000, as against 2 127 000 for the USA. However, if this is divided, as in figure 1.2, so that personnel available to fight in a war are distinguished from others, the apparent imbalance vanishes.

Figure 1.2   Adjusted Comparison of Soviet and US Military Personnel 1976 (in 000s)

Soviet Total	4800	American Total	2127
minus Internal Security and			
Border Guards	(430)	minus Chaplains and	
		Construction	(3)
Construction Troops	(250)	Far East Troops	(115)
Military working on			
farms and railways	(150)		
Political Officers	(70)		
Civil Defence	(20)		
Supply, Storage and			
R & D Troops[1]	(170)		
Coast Guard	(60)		
Sino-Soviet Border			
Troops	(500)		
Czech Garrison	(55)		
Other civilians in			
uniform	(300)		
Sub-total	2795		
minus Extra Air Defence			
Troops[2]	(475)		
Extra Strategic			
Forces Troops[2]	(275)		
Adjusted Soviet Total	**2045**	**Adjusted American Total**	**2009**

1. R & D: Research and Development
2. In these two missions the USSR maintains more personnel than the USA; believing that the excess implies no extra threat to the USA, Aspin has adjusted them out of his comparison.

Source: Dan Smith *The Defence of the Realm in the 1980s*[3] p78 from the Defence Intelligence Agency.

Taking the International Institute of Strategic Studies (IISS) estimates of personnel as a starting point, we can proceed with some sort of comparison.[6] Figure 1.3 shows NATO and WP troops in rough balance overall. There is, however, another ambiguity here which may confuse. France is politically in NATO, and has troops stationed in Germany, but French troops are not under NATO command. Whether to include or exclude France from NATO in these comparisons requires an analysis of how France would act in a given situation. On the WP side, it is doubtful whether some of the Eastern European armies could be relied on to participate in an attack on the West. Poland, Romania and Czechoslovakia might for instance fall into this category. Nield[8] shows how making opposite extreme assumptions on these questions radically alters how the balance is perceived. For example one extreme assumption leads to concluding a NATO advantage of 42 divisions to 6, where the opposite extreme gives the WP an advantage of 46 divisions to 27. This important problem also bears on comparisons of other aspects of military capability.

14

Figure 1.3 Total NATO and WP Armed Forces 1980 (in 000s)

WP		NATO	
Bulgaria	149.0	Belgium	87.9
Czechslovakia	195.0	Britain	329.2
East Germany	162.0	Canada	78.6
Hungary	93.0	Denmark	35.1
Poland	317.5	West Germany	495.0
Romania	184.5	Greece	181.5
USSR[1]	3568.0	Italy	366.0
		Luxembourg	0.7
		Netherlands	115.0
		Norway	37.0
		Portugal	59.5
		Turkey	567.0
		USA	2050.0
TOTAL	4669.0	TOTAL	4407.5

1. The USSR figure excludes "uniformed civilians"
Source: *The Military Balance 1980-81*[5]

A superiority in numbers would in any case give military superiority only in certain circumstances. Traditional military wisdom has it that a superiority of 3 to 1 is necessary for an attack to succeed. While this 3 to 1 rule has many provisos (the important question of armaments will be discussed next), it does indicate that a defending army has a natural advantage over an attacking army.[9] For an alliance seeking only defence capability, a mild imbalance should thus not be alarming.

It may be that the size of armed forces in both NATO and WP countries reflects needs quite different from fighting each other. National armies may be involved in fighting regional wars, policing their own spheres of influence, maintaining a regime against internal dissent, or "teaching young people discipline". In some cases these roles are obvious; for instance the reduction in Portugal's armed forces in the 1970s was clearly a result of Portugal's disengagement from Africa, and had little effect on NATO's ability to fight the WP. Nearer home, the presence of thousands of British troops in Northern Ireland shows that personnel figures do not simply reflect preparedness for global nuclear conflict.

1.5 THE BALANCE OF CONVENTIONAL ARMS

In modern warfare it is the effectiveness of armaments, rather than the cost or the numbers of troops operating them which is the most important. Thus comparisons of armaments available to NATO and the WP should help us to make a more valid assessment of their relative capabilities for war. Yet once again we encounter the problems of what should be included and of lack of access to data because of government secrecy. Here, in addition, there is the problem of how to interpret statistics in the light of which "war scenarios" are considered to be likely. One crucial problem is the tendency for available statistics to consider total numbers of aircraft or other forms of

Figure: 1.4 Comparison of Selected NATO and WP Forces in Europe 1969, 1973, 1978

	NORTHERN AND CENTRAL[1]					
	1969		1973		1978	
	NATO	WP	NATO	WP	NATO	WP
Manpower (000s)	600	925	600	900	626	943
Tanks (000s)	5.25	12.5	6.5	17	7	21.1
Tactical aircraft:	2050	3795	1890	4300	2375	4055
Light bombers	50	260	140	250	160	130
Fighter/ground attack	1150	1285	1100	1400	1400	1350
Interceptors	450	2000	350	2100	435	2025
Reconnaissance	400	250	300	550	380	550

	SOUTHERN[1]					
	1969		1973		1978	
	NATO	WP	NATO	WP	NATO	WP
Manpower (000s)	525	375	530	320	550	388
Tanks (000s)	1.8	4.6	2.15	6.2	4.3	6.8
Tactical aircraft:	975	1185	856	1195	938	1645
Light bombers	—	60	6	30	—	50
Fighter/ground attack	550	215	450	125	628	375
Interceptors	300	860	275	950	220	1000
Reconnaissance	125	50	125	90	90	220

	TOTAL[1]					
	1969		1973		1978	
	NATO	WP	NATO	WP	NATO	WP
Manpower (000s)	1125	1300	1130	1220	1176	1331
Tanks (000s)	7.05	17.1	8.65	23.2	11.3	27.9
Tactical aircraft:	3025	4980	2746	5495	3313	5700
Light bombers	50	320	146	280	160	180
Fighter/ground attack	1700	1500	1550	1525	2028	1725
Interceptors	750	2860	625	3050	655	3025
Reconnaissance	525	300	425	640	470	770

1. For NATO, the 'Total' area is the area of SACEUR's command. All French forces, and British ground forces in Britain, are excluded. WP figures for 'Northern and Central' include the forces of Czechoslovakia, the German Democratic Republic and Poland, Soviet forces stationed in those countries, and most forces in western USSR. WP figures for 'Southern' include the forces of Bulgaria, Hungary and Romania, Soviet forces stationed in Hungary and in south-western USSR.

Source: Dan Smith *The Defence of the Realm* p72

military equipment, without any regard for their various capabilities. Thus questions of range, accuracy, reliability, vulnerability, etc. are omitted, making interpretation difficult. A particular example is that of tanks. It is often claimed that an overwhelming Soviet advantage in numbers of tanks (noted in figure 1.4) makes it necessary for NATO to deploy new weapons.

The data presented neglect the fact that NATO tends to scrap old tanks when it acquires new ones, while WP countries usually keep old obsolete tanks as well as other newer ones. In addition, measurements are often inaccurate. Western estimates of WP tanks used to be made by counting tank sheds from the air, until it was found that many of these sheds were empty. It is furthermore difficult to see why the deficiency in tanks should necessarily be a disadvantage to a defending army. NATO has a strategy based on lighter more mobile vehicles and large numbers of very sophisticated anti-tank weapons, so a "balance" of tanks would not be expected.

The more developed technology of the west, in particular its micro-electronics technology, has a great impact on the quality of its weapons. The chairman of the Joint Chiefs of Staffs of the USA noted in 1978 that "Science and technology have been among the principal factors in continued overall military superiority".[10] Thus, as can be seen in figure 1.4, while the WP has *more* aircraft than NATO, it does not necessarily have a greater capability. Indeed a Pentagon study reported in 1973[11] that overall, NATO's conventional forces in Europe were superior to those of the WP, despite the fact that according to the crude numerical comparisons shown in table 1.4 WP forces were better staffed and equipped. This numerical imbalance shifted only slightly in the WP's favour between 1973 and 1978 and no major changes have occurred since then.

The conclusions of more recent Pentagon reports have tended towards the now more politically expedient conclusion that NATO lags behind in this area. As we have seen, it is difficult to match this change in public attitude to statistical evidence of real changes in military effectiveness.

1.6 THE BALANCE OF NUCLEAR ARMS

Henry Kissinger once commented "What in the name of God is a strategic superiority? What do you do with it?".[12] According to the concept of MAD, once enough nuclear weapons are available to destroy an enemy's cities, more weapons are unnecessary. However, new nuclear weapons *are* being developed. The available statistics may help to tell us why and to what effect.

Nuclear weapons have changed since their introduction in the 1940s and 1950s. We have referred to the early diversification of strategic weapons into the "strategic triad" of bombers, ICBM's and SLBM's and to the deployment of "tactical" nuclear weapons. Following these developments there have been substantial increases in the numbers and qualitative changes in the capabilities of these weapons. Also intermediate weapons have been introduced to meet the claimed need for "flexible response".

Figure 1.5 shows the capabilities of most of the missiles deployed by NATO and the WP in the 1970s and projected for the 1980s. A more detailed description of these and other nuclear weapons is available elsewhere.[13] In interpreting the data in the figure the following comments may prove useful.
(i) Information is not available about the USSR's plans for acquiring new weapons.
(ii) The table has been divided into "strategic" and "Eurostrategic" weapons, though this distinction is hazy. The Pershing II and Ground Launched Cruise Missile (GLCM)

Figure 1.5 Principal Strategic and Eurostrategic Missiles

of each	Type	Name	Year introduced	Number of MIRVs	Power of each warhead kilotons	Range each km	CEP m	Lethality warhead[1]
Strategic								
US	ICBM	Titan II	1963	1	9000	11500	1300	40
		Minuteman II	1966	1	2000	13000	400	100
		Minuteman III	1970	3	170	13000	300	30
		Minuteman III with Mk 12A	1970	3	350	13000	200	100
		MX	proj	10	350	13000	100[2]	500
	SLBM	Polaris-A3	1964	1	600	4500	900	4
		Poseidon-C3	1970	10	50	7500	500	5
		Trident I	1980	8	100	7500	500	10
		Trident II	proj	14	150	11000	500[2]	10
	ALCM	—	proj	1	200	1800	30-90	400-4000
USSR	ICBM	SS-9	1966	1	18000	12000	1000	70
		SS-11	1966	1	1000	10500	1500	4
		SS-13	1969	1	1000	8000	1300	6
		SS-17	1977	4	900	9000	300-600	30-100
		SS-18	1976	8	2000	10000	300-600	40-200
		SS-19	1976	6	500	9000	300-450	30-70
	SLBM	SS-N-6	1968	1	1000	3000	2000	2
		SS-N-8	1973	1	1000	8000	1000	10
		SS-N-18	—	3	1000	7500	600	30
	ALCM	AS-3	1961	1	1000	3500	—	—
Eurostrategic								
US	BM	Pershing IA	1962	1	60-400	750	450	8-30
		Pershing II	proj	1	10-20	1600	45	200-400
	GLCM	Tomahawk	proj	1	200	2500	30-90	400-4000
USSR	BM	SS-4	1959	1	1000	3000	2400	2
		SS-5	1959	1	1000	3700	1250	6
		SS-12	1969	1	1000	800	—	—
		SS-20	1977	3	150	4000	400	18
	SLBM	SS-N-5	1964	1	1000	1200	—	—
UK	SLBM	Polaris-A3	1967	1	600	4500	900	4
France	SLBM	S-3	1971	1	150	3000	—	—
	BM	M-20	1977	1	1000	5000	—	—

1. Units – (kilotons) $^{2/3}$ (metres) $^{-2}$ X 10^5
2. Terminal Guidance systems systems are known to be being developed for these missiles. If these are deployed, the CEP will reduce to a few tens of metres.
3. In the case of ALCMs the range of the carrying aircraft should be added to this figure.

Sources: IISS - *The Military Balance 1980-81*
SIPRI - *Yearbook 1980*

would for instance be capable of penetrating quite far into Soviet Territory.

(iii) In addition to the missiles in figure 1.5, free falling nuclear bombs and Short Range Attack Missiles (SRAMs) are available for many of the WP and NATO aircraft. Apart from the B52 with Air Launched Cruise Missiles (ALCM), and the Tupelov Bear with the "kangaroo" missiles (AS-3) (a much less sophisticated ALCM, one carried per aircraft) long range aircraft are presently too vulnerable to present a threat to the superpower homelands to compare with that of ground and sea launched missiles. The development of more sophisticated aircraft, such as the American B1, may shortly change this.

(iv) Most modern missiles are fitted with Multiple Independently targetable Re-entry Vehicles (MIRVs). These allow one missile to destroy several targets. The number of MIRVs on each missile is noted on the figure.

(v) The accuracy of missiles is generally measured by the radius of the circle around the target within which half the number of warheads aimed at that target would on average fall. This is called the Circular Error Probable (CEP). The range and CEP for missiles given in the figures are of course estimates subject to error.

(vi) "Lethality" is a measure of the ability of a weapon to destroy a specific small target for example a missile silo. This ability depends on accuracy and explosive power according to the formula:

$$\text{Lethality} = (\text{explosive power})^{2/3}/(\text{CEP})^2$$

The concept of lethality is explained further in "Towards the final abyss".[14]

Despite the uncertainties in estimating some of the quantities shown in the Figure, some trends in missile capabilities are clear:

First, by looking at the CEP's of missiles against the year introduced, it can be seen that missiles are becoming much more accurate. This is especially so for the USA who hold a clear lead in missile accuracy.

Second, it is clear that more MIRVs are now being fitted to missiles. This trend is also shown in Figure 1.6, which shows the total number of ICBMs deployed by each of the super-powers, and the total number of independently targetable warheads. Missile numbers can be seen to have kept steady (regulated by SALT), while warhead numbers have greatly increased. The SALT agreement, if adhered to, allows up to 10 MIRVs on each missile, fewer on some.

Thirdly, as a consequence of the increased accuracy of missiles, and despite the fact that after MIRVing individual warheads are now less powerful, lethality of modern warheads is very much higher than that of older weapons. Here also the USA is seen to have a clear lead.

One implication of these two trends is that a strategy of attempting to destroy the enemy's delivery vehicles before they are launched (counterforce strategy), rather than relying on the threat to destroy cities to deter an attack (countercity strategy), becomes increasingly viable. For a counterforce missile salvo against the enemy's missiles to be effective, available warheads must be accurate and powerful (have high "lethality") and be numerous enough to destroy most enemy missiles. The superpowers have embarked on a race to improve capabilities and numbers on the one hand, and to improve missile invulnerability on the other. This race is now becoming increasingly unstable following qualitative improvements in accuracy, and hence lethality. The cruise missile, either air-launched (ALCM) or ground-launched (GLCM), is, because of its accuracy, extremely lethal. Though slower moving, it is very hard to detect with radar. It is possible, therefore, that it could be used as a counterforce weapon. The deployment of ALCMs and GLCMs in the quantities currently planned (3400 ALCM and 460 GLCM) would, if this was the case, greatly increase any US counterforce threat to the USSR. A

Figure 1.6 Numbers of Strategic Missiles and Warheads 1971-1980 USA and USSR

		Year									
		1971	1972	1973	1974	1975	1976	1977	1978	1979	1980
ICBM	USA	1054	1054	1054	1054	1054	1054	1054	1054	1054	1054
	USSR	1527	1527	1547	1567	1587	1547	1447	1400	1398	1398
Warheads	USA	2938	3858	5210	5678	6410	6842	7130	7274	7274	7258
	USSR	1887	1986	2114	2222	2302	2758	3508	4427	5375	6266

Sources: *The Military Balance*[6]
               SIPRI Yearbook[7]

power threatened by a counterforce attack is likely to adopt a "launch on warning" strategy to prevent its missiles being destroyed. With such a strategy the chances of launching missiles in error would clearly be increased.

It is clear from the statistics presented that the USA possesses a much stronger counterforce capability than the USSR. In fact neither superpower has anything approaching a credible threat of destroying a sufficient proportion of the other's missiles in a pre-emptive strike to prevent a devastating countercity retaliation. The trend, though, is unmistakably towards this situation, with the USA having a clear advantage in this race. Improvements in Anti-Submarine Warfare technology, especially for the USA, mean that missile-carrying submarines can no longer be regarded as invulnerable.[15] All three corners of the "strategic" triad may soon be vulnerable to a first strike counterforce threat.

In October 1981 President Reagan decided to proceed with the B1 bomber development and MX missile deployment. This will increase the USA's counterforce strength through improved weapon capabilities, notably the great accuracy and high number of MIRVs on the MX missile. Reagan decided though, that the MX missiles should be housed in old silos, rather than in the much more difficult to destroy system of new silos linked by underground tracks. It may be noted that the abandoned project would have the effect of increasing missile invulnerability without adding to counterforce potential. Thus the USA may be dropping the least destabilising item of its program.

1.7 THE NUCLEAR BALANCE IN EUROPE

One of the arguments commonly produced to support the deployment of GLCMs and Pershing IIs in Europe is that the WP has an enormous advantage over NATO in nuclear weapons in Europe which it is necessary to redress. Apart from the importance of this question in its own right, the way statistics are used in this argument provides examples of many of the issues which we have considered earlier in this chapter.

The 1981 Defence White Paper[16] presented the data shown in Figure 1.7 in support of statements that NATO is at a disadvantage. We will look at the assumptions behind this interpretation of the situation point by point.

(i) SLBMs are not included in the Figure. France and Britain have 80 and 64 SLBMs respectively compared with the 69 which the USSR assigns to the European theatre. In addition to British and French weapons are the 45 Poseidon missiles which the USA allocates for use in Europe.

(ii) The data in Figure 1.7 are counts of delivery systems rather than warheads. A missile with MIRVs is clearly more potent than one without. Aircraft will vary in the number of short range attack missiles (SRAMs) on nuclear bombs which they can carry.

(iii) The USSR, unlike NATO, does not keep short-range nuclear missiles and nuclear artillery in Eastern Europe. There *is* a stockpile of such weapons kept in Russia, but these would not be available for a surprise attack, since their transport to the East/West border could not go unnoticed.

(iv) The effectiveness of the weapons are not considered. Some aircraft are much more likely to reach their targets than others, and missiles vary in their reliability.

(v) Considering the balance of "Eurostrategic" nuclear weapons out of the context of a comparison of "strategic" weapons strengths only makes sense if the flexible response

Figure 1.7 The Nuclear Balance in Europe according to the 1981 Defence White Paper[16]

	WP			NATO		
	Missiles	Aircraft	Total	Missiles	Aircraft	Total
Long range	540	350	890	18	260	278
Medium range	650	2000	2650	180	700	880
Short range	950[1]		950	1200[1]		1200

1. Including Nuclear capable artillery.
Source: *Defence White Paper 1981*[16].

Figure 1.8 Balance of Long and Medium range Nuclear Weapons in Europe according to the IISS[5]

	WP		NATO	
	Warheads available	Arriving warheads	Warheads available	Arriving warheads
Ballistic Missile Warheads	1040	540	642	433
Air-Delivered Warheads	955	279	526	122
Total	1995	819	1168	555

Source: *The Military Balance 1980-81*[5]

doctrine is accepted. The capability for MAD is assured for both alliances by their arsenals of strategic weapons. It can be seen from figure 1.6 that the addition of European weapons to the strategic totals would make little difference to the overall balance. It might also be noted that the strategic weapons could, of course, be targetted equally well on Europe as on the USSR or USA.

(vi) The balance of nuclear weapons in Europe has little bearing on arguments concerning the claimed need, in the case of Britain and France, for an "independent nuclear deterrent". Supporters of such a claim would have to give evidence of situations in which the threat of their use "independently" (i.e. outside NATO) would be effective. Only if such an explanation could be produced could arguments about "balance" be meaningful, since only then would the composition of the "sides' be known.

In *The Military Balance 1980-81* the International Institute of Strategic Studies attempts to make a comparison for Long and Medium range weapons taking some of the above points into consideration. Numbers of "arriving warheads" are calculated taking into account "survivability" (likelihood of being shot down), and "reliability" (likelihood of system functioning as planned after launch) among other factors. The estimates from this procedure (including the 45 Poseidon missiles) are summarised in Figure 1.8. This still indicates an overall WP lead of 819 to 555, but is a long way from the "three to one" advantage suggested by the White Paper. This comparison only includes weapons with ranges over 160 km.

Even if Soviet warheads kept in the USSR are included, NATO has a considerable lead in "short range" nuclear warheads. If the "Enhanced radiation warhead" or neutron bomb is added to NATO's arsenal, this lead will increase. If an analysis of "arriving warheads" were done for *all* nuclear weapons assigned for use in Europe, there is little doubt that, for what it is worth, NATO's total would surpass that of the WP.

1.8 CONCLUSIONS

It is clear that in discussing the balance of power between NATO and the WP, governments and the media are able to select the statistics which suit their case best. It is, therefore, necessary to approach any statistics critically. Two important questions to have in the back of our minds are:–

(i) Is like being compared with like? Examples of invalid comparisons already considered include comparison of obsolete arms with modern technologically superior arms, and of combat troops with border guards.

(ii) Does a specific imbalance matter? We have seen that a tank force need not be matched by tanks, but may be countered by anti-tank weapons. It is even harder to make sense of the idea of a strategic superiority in nuclear weapons, let alone infer this from relative capabilities (e.g. imbalances in numbers of a particular sort of weapon).

Despite our criticisms of, and reservations about the data available to us, the following three important conclusions can be drawn from them:–

(i) It is often argued that the WP holds a superiority over NATO in conventional forces which would allow it to make a credible threat of an attack on Western Europe. We see no convincing statistical evidence for this.

(ii) While there is evidence of a WP lead in Long and Medium range nuclear capability in Europe, this is very much less than we are often lead to believe. For short range weapons and Strategic Nuclear Warheads, NATO has a lead over the WP.

(iii) There is a trend in nuclear weapons towards more accurate and more numerous delivery vehicles. This trend constitutes a move towards a situation in which a power might feel threatened by a first strike against its missiles. The USA has, at present and potentially, a very clear superiority in this field.

References

1. *UK Government. Statement on Defence Estimates 1981* Vol 2 Table 2.3. London: HMSO 1981.
2. *Armaments and Disarmament Information Unit Bulletin.* August 1979.
3. Quoted in: UN Secretary General. *A comprehensive study of Nuclear Weapons.* New York: United Nations 1980.
4. Smith D. *The defence of the Realm.* London Croom Helm 1980.
5. Thompson, E.P. and Smith D. *Protest and Survive.* London: Penguin 1979.
6. International Institute of Strategic Studies. *The Military Balance.* London: IISS 1980.
7. Stockholm International Peace Research Institute. *SIPRI Year Book of World Armaments and Disarmament 1981.* Taylor and Francis London 1980.
8. Nield R. *How to make your mind up about the bomb.* London: Deutsch 1981. (Note that comparisons of personnel by divisions is problematic as the size of divisions varies from army to army.)
9. Enthoven, A. and Smith, K.W. *How much is enough? Shaping the defence program 1961-69.* New York: Harper and Row 1971.
10. Brown General G.S. *United States military posture for FY 1979* p.105. Washington: US Department of Defence 1978.
11. Cook, R. and Smith, D. *What future in NATO?* London: Fabian Society 1978.
12. Reported in The Guardian 17 March 1971.
13. Rogers, P. *A guide to Nuclear Weapons.* London: Housmans 1981.
14. Pentz, M. *Towards the final Abyss.* London: J.D. Bernal Peace Library 1980.
15. Wit, J.S. Advances in Anti-Submarine Warfare. *Scientific American 244*, p27-37. Feb. 1981.
16. *UK Government Statement on Defence Estimates 1981.* Vol.1. London: HMSO 1981.

2 THE WIDER CONTEXT

2.1 TOWARDS A NUCLEAR WORLD?

We have surveyed the "balance of terror" that is the build-up of nuclear weapons on the part of the Eastern and Western military alliances, the WP and NATO. But even today there are countries belonging to neither alliance which have built and tested nuclear devices. Furthermore, many more countries are capable of doing so and the number involved is growing.

Figure 2.1 presents information on this state of affairs. As with other nuclear statistics, there must be some uncertainty and doubt concerning the real position of some countries. For example, it has been claimed that South Africa, as well as capable of building a nuclear device, has actually tested one, though this remains controversial. Brazil has denied supplying nuclear materials to Iraq but evidence accumulated following the Israeli attack on Iraq's "peaceful" nuclear station in 1981 suggested otherwise. It is evident that many countries would wish the real state of affairs to remain obscure, both concerning their own capabilities and their dealings with other countries; therefore figure 2.1 probably understates nuclear links.

It seems that, unless present trends are reversed, over thirty states will possess nuclear weapons by the end of the 1980s. What does this mean in terms of human security? The total power of the bombs dropped in World War II was around 2 megatonnes – in six years. The global nuclear armoury can be put conservatively at anywhere between 10 000 and 15 000 megatonnes, in around 50 000 warheads[1] and still higher estimates have been given.[2] As often noted, this is enough to kill the human race several times over, if deployed for this purpose. Between 1945 and 1980 there were 1271 nuclear tests, 783 of which occured after the signing of the *Partial Test Ban Treaty* in 1963.

In figure 2.1 we also present material on the proliferation of nuclear energy systems. While the "peaceful atom" is cited as a reason for developing power stations, there is substantial evidence to support the view that nuclear power and nuclear weapons are closely linked. Even were nuclear programmes not designed for military purposes, it should be borne in mind that the proliferation of reactors makes more possible a spread of nuclear materials for use by states or terrorist groups and that reactors are likely candidates for attack in conventional war and terrorist activity. In the late 1970s there was evidence that earlier forecasts of nuclear generating capacity were overstated, with many plans remaining on paper. SIPRI estimates of plants operable, under construction or ordered are therefore likely to be too high and we confine ourselves here to covering only commercial power stations operational by the end of 1980. Because the figures in figure 2.1 exclude power stations of a purely research or prototype nature and, in particular, do *not* cover military reactors, they definitely understate the case. However, civilian power stations are significant in that they are large and difficult to conceal and are thus likely to be obvious targets. According to nuclear industry sources a further 200 commercial stations are in the planning stage in addition to the 300 or so already in operation.

Figure 2.1 Nuclear Proliferation

Nuclear devices by country as of mid 1981	Source of Equipment and Materials	Commercial Nuclear Power Stations in Operation at end of 1980
Devices built and tested:		
USA		73
USSR		32
UK		23
France		17
China		—
India		5
Capable of Building:		
Canada	contributed to Allied war effort	10
Federal Republic of Germany	US USSR	6
Israel	US	n.a.
Italy	US UK	4
Japan	US UK Australia	22
Pakistan	US, Switzerland, ?W.European firms ?Turkey ?China	1
South Africa	US, France, ?Israel other NATO	—
Sweden	US	8
Switzerland	US FRG	4
Capable of Building in 6 years:		
Argentina	FRG, Switzerland, Canada	—
Australia	US UK	—
Austria	US FRG	1
Belgium	US France	—
Brazil	FRG ?Iraq	—
Denmark	US	6

Iraq	France, Italy, ?Brazil	—
South Korea	US Canada, France	—
Netherlands	US FRG	n.a.
Norway	US FRG	1
Spain	US UK France	2
Taiwan	US Canada	—
Turkey?	?Pakistan	—

Capable of Building in 10 years:

Egypt	US USSR	4
Finland	USSR Sweden	2
Libya	USSR ?Pakistan	—
Yugoslavia	US USSR	4

No Apparent Nuclear Weapons Capability, but Using or Planning Reactors:

East Germany		5
Czechoslovakia		3
Bulgaria		3
Cuba		—
Iran	(Programme closed in 1979 revolution)	
Mexico		—
Poland		—
Philippines		—
Romania		—
Thailand		—

Source: Columns 1 and 2 from *Newsweek* (June 22 1981, p19) and subsequent press sources.
Column 3 based on data from *Nuclear News wall chart* (Sept 1980) *'Commercial Nuclear Power Stations Around the World'*, *Nucleonics Week* (22(3) January 1981), SANE Third World First *Nuclear Links*, (1981, SANE/TWF), and using advice provided by Gordon McKerron and Steve Thomas.

This has led to a situation when almost thirty Third World countries have achieved access to parts of the nuclear fuel cycle. Co-operation between these countries can bring together the ingredients of nuclear weapons. The concentration of energy research on nuclear power will tend to increase nuclear proliferation, though energy research consumes less than a fifth of the sums spent on military research.[3] International energy agency member countries spent in 1978 some 7 billion US dollars on energy research. According to data cited in *World Military and Social Expenditures*[4] of this $3.7 billion went to nuclear energy; a mere $400 million went to conservation, with less than $3 billion to other energy sources and supporting systems.

Compared to many Western countries, Britain seems to have a relatively restrained role in the process of nuclear proliferation. One nuclear link, however, has given particular cause for concern. This is the link that exists with South Africa through the Rossing uranium mine in Namibia. Dan Smith[5] has assembled valuable information on this topic. He reveals that a British multinational – Rio Tinto Zinc – is a 25% shareholder in the mine, making it the largest foreign shareholder. (Lord Carrington only relinquished his directorship of Rio Tinto Zinc when he became Britain's Foreign Secretary.) Britain is the largest foreign purchaser of uranium, buying about 25% of output between 1977-82; this is the largest source of supply for our domestic nuclear programme. Apart from the financial support this provides for apartheid, and the shoring up of the illegal occupation of Namibia, Britain is thus indirectly aiding South Africa in its development of nuclear weapons.

It is clear that nuclear proliferation is making the whole world more dangerous as countries other than NATO and WP countries achieve the capability to wage nuclear war.

2.2   36 YEARS OF "PEACE"?

It has been argued that military expenditure, particularly that sustaining the nuclear balance of terror, has helped bring the world in general greater security. Certainly Western Europe has had little experience of war since World War II, although by some definitions events in Northern Ireland constitute war. However, to assess the truth of the argument we must look at the global picture. Firstly we must establish what constitutes a "war" as this is not generally defined, although most researchers agree concerning major conflicts and about the overall trends and regional distribution of warfare. The data presented in figure 2.2 is based on a definition of wars as involving conflict between the armed forces of different countries on one or other's territories. It excludes minor border clashes and civil wars.

Figure 2.2 gives details on some 120 wars occurring between 1945 and 1976. (By way of comparison Sivard notes 111 wars between 1960 and 1980.) It is evident that war has been more frequent in the third world, particularly in Asia and the Middle East. These regions have also seen enormous increases in the number of refugees, accounting for the majority of the rise in the number recorded from 7.9 million in 1964 to 16 million in 1979.[4]

The evidence is therefore that the world has not been peaceful since World War II and that there have been more wars in the Third World where military expenditure has grown proportionately faster. Furthermore, the data presented does not isolate those wars in the Third World countries where the super-powers have also been involved, in indirect confrontation with each other.

Figure 2.2 Wars in Different World Regions 1945-76[1]

	Number of wars	Percentage of world total	Percentage of total duration of wars
Europe	5	4.2	3.8
Asia	35	29.2	40.7
Middle East (incl Asiatic & African Arab territories)	36	30.0	19.4
Sub-Saharan Africa	21	17.5	25.5
Latin America	23	19.2	10.6

1. "Wars" includes "peace-keeping" interactions, but excludes internal civil wars like Biafra, Northern Ireland.
Source: I. Kende (1977) *'Dynamics of Wars...' Instant Research on Peace and Violence 2/1977*

2.3 WORLD RESOURCES CONSUMED BY THE MILITARY

Statistics can help us outline the background of world military spending within which nuclear proliferation is taking place. They also demonstrate the extent to which the world's resources are being wasted on weapons and armies.

Figure 2.3 presents basic data on world military expenditure .[4] We have already noted some of the problems in interpreting such data and in choosing between the figures provided by different sources. In one SIPRI study,[6] various estimates of military expenditures for particular countries were compared. 29 countries gave estimates

Figure 2.3   World Military Expenditure

	1960			1978		
	"Poor" countries	"Rich" countries	World total	"Poor" countries	"Rich" countries	World total
Military expenditure: 000s $ million[1]	21	195	216	87	288	375
As a percentage of total economic output (GNP)	3.4	6.8	6.2	4.9	4.6	4.7

1. adjusted for inflation
Source: *Estimates in Sivard 1980.*

varying by 0-7%, 39 countries gave estimates varying by between 7 and 15% and the estimates of 37 countries varied by more than 15% (including Libya, where estimates varied by over 80%). Sivard's data in figure 2.3 groups countries into "rich" and "poor" and these groupings hopefully "smooth over" some of the inaccuracies here, although the reliability of all these figures is ultimately suspect. What do the data of figure 2.3 suggest? First, that world military expenditure has increased substantially in recent decades. Second, that rich countries account for the lions' share of this, although poor countries have been increasing their expenditure more rapidly. Third, that in the wake of the Cold War, rich countries generally reduced the *relative* importance of military expenditure in their economies (see the lower part of the table). In fact, this is largely accounted for by a decline in the proportion of resources that the USA devoted to its military, which brought it closer in that respect during the 1970s to the rest of NATO.

Whether the relative decline will continue is a matter of doubt. SIPRI estimated that in 1980 there was a rise in the proportion of world output consumed by the military to some 6%.[7] NATO countries have resolved to increase military expenditure in real terms over the next few years, although growth in output is anticipated to be low. However, problems are being found in meeting the 3% increase (in real terms) objective in many European countries. The scale of the US expenditure makes it likely that the war drive in that country will be important in global terms.

The current levels of military expenditure are equal to the recorded income of the poorest half of the world's population. As Blackaby[3] notes, military expenditure runs at about a million dollars a minute: and as for the consumption of physical resources, the US military alone consumes annually more oil than all of South Asia, and vast quantities of other materials – some 40% of the total US consumption of titanium, and about 10% of its aluminium, chromium, copper, iron, lead, molybdenum, manganese, nickel, tin and zinc.

Human resources are also consumed. Data on "armed forces" are somewhat suspect, because there are many paramilitary forces which escape inclusion and the data in figure 2.4 may underestimate the state of affairs. However the figure shows a growth in military personnel since 1960 and demonstrates that the number of armed forces in the world today is somewhat larger than Britain's adult male population.

Compared to figure 2.3 the growth in the number of armed forces has been slower than that in the money spent on the military: 1.5% as compared to 3.9% per year on the average over the 1960s and 70s. It is likely that this, rather than representing higher wages, reflects a growing capital-intensity of the military – each soldier being equipped with more, and more lethal weaponry.

Figure 2.4   World Armed Forces

	1960			1978		
	"Poor" countries	"Rich" countries	World total	"Poor" countries	"Rich" countries	World total
Armed Forces: millions	8.7	9.6	18.6	14.3	9.5	23.8
per thousand population	4.0	11.2	6.1	4.3	9.1	5.5

Source: *Estimates in Sivard 1980*

While these data tell us about the quantity of people employed in the military, they tell us little about the activities they are engaged in. It would be interesting to know too, about the consequences of military-type discipline on both conscripts and volunteers. In late 1978, some 44 countries were under military regimes, or had experienced military coups or interventions since 1960.[8] Among these are several nations which are near nuclear powers according to figure 2.1: Pakistan, Argentina, Brazil, and so on. Other nuclear powers – South Africa, for example – are only able to maintain their extremely explosive internal regimes by military force directed against internal dissidents and guerilpas based in neighbouring territories. (This latter 'overspill' is among the main sources of international conflict in the regions in question).

2.4 ARMS TRADE

The rich countries of the world, Britain among them, are doubly involved in the arms race, not only by being direct participants, but also by being heavily involved in the arms trade. The profits that can be made from the arms trade, if not fuelling the arms race, would certainly lead to considerable opposition to any attempt to reduce armaments.

The arms trade, and the associated profits, have grown considerably over recent decades. Figure 2.5 presents data on this, and as usual we can draw some conclusions from the data although still needing to utter some words of caution. Once again, these data are likely to substantially underestimate the scale of international military sales. First, many sales of weapons – especially small arms – are simply unrecorded: the Campaign Against the Arms Trade has claimed that these sales constitute a sizeable fraction of the recorded sales. Second, many apparently civilian projects – radar for airports, road construction, trucks – are actually intended for military purposes. Some of the most sophisticated equipment falls into this latter category, and it is here that much nuclear-related power technology may be traded, as in the relatively visible case of power stations.

Figure 2.5   World Trade in Arms

	1960			1978		
	"Poor" countries	"Rich" countries	World total	"Poor" countries	"Rich" countries	World total
Arms imports: 000s $ millions[1]	1.1	1.3	2.4	13.6	4.9	20.5
Balance of Arms Trade in favour of rich countries 000s $ millions[1]	—	1.0	—	—	15.0	—

1.   Current prices

Source: *Estimates in Sivard 1980*

31

Figure 2.6   Britain and the Arms Trade

Figure 2.6(a)

£ million

	1980	
	exports	imports
Armoured fighting vehicles and parts	50	7
Combat aircraft including helicopters[1]	40	2
Military non-combat aircraft including helicopters[1]	64	—
Military aircraft including helicopters, other than newly constructed	66	—
Warships including air cushion vehicles	59	–
Guns, small arms and parts	64	32
Guided weapons and missiles	25	65
Ammunition	102	20
Radio communications and radar apparatus	55	19
Optical equipment and training simulators	12	2
Identified defence equipment[2]: total	537	147
of which		
NATO countries and other W Europe	111	137
Middle East and N African countries	158	1
Sub-Saharan Africa	121	3
Latin America and Caribbean	13	1
Asia and Far East	134	5

1. Newly constructed only
2. Categories of equipment which can be identified through the Customs and Excise Tariff. In addition there are substantial exports of defence equipment which it is not possible to distinguish from similar goods for civilian purposes in the Customs records. However, information is available from the Society of British Aerospace Companies and individual electronics and motor vehicle manufacturing companies which gives rise to the following estimates for these items:

Figure 2.6(b)

£ million

	1979 exports
Military airframe parts[1]	191
Military aeroengines and parts[1]	85
Military aircraft equipment[2]	1140
Military space equipment	11
Other military road vehicles	90

1. The exports of aircraft parts, aeroengines and aeroengine parts in connection with international collaborative projects are excluded.
2. Other than military airborne radars and ground flying trainers, which are identified through the Tariff and included in Figure 2.6(a).

Source: *Statement on the Defence Estimates, 2* (Defence Statistics) 1980 HMSO.

Figure 2.5 does make clear the increase in the overall level of arms trade, especially that from rich to poor countries. Accordingly to ACDA, whose estimates, as we note in the Appendix must be treated with some caution, the main exporters in the late 1970s were the USA and USSR (each exporting around $7 billion of arms), with France and the U.K following with sales of more than $1 billion each. The Middle East, not surprisingly, was the main importer, followed by Africa whose arms purchases mushroomed in the 1970s.[9]

Figure 2.6 focusses on Britain's contribution to the trade in arms. Britain makes a clear balance of payments surplus in this field, although more is purchased from NATO and W. European countries than is sold to them. Again this figure underestimates the situation, for these data exclude items of various types due to being based on customs and excise (i.e. tariff) statistics. Apart from undeclared and smuggled items there are components of military goods (such as aircraft engines) which are not distinguished from similar civilian components. Data on exports for some of these items is available, as shown in figure 2.6(b). (These export figures are lower than the figure that might be obtained for military orders, but these latter are unstable and subject to eventual inflation.) We shall see later, however, that "our" balance of trade surplus is offset by Britain's overseas military expenditure.

The arms trade has received substantial support from successive governments. When Secretary for Defence, Denis Healey, set up the Defence Sales Organisation in 1966, he proclaimed that:

> "While the Government attaches the highest importance to making progress in the field of arms control and disarmament, we must also take what practical steps we can to ensure that this country does not fail to secure its rightful share of the valuable commercial market".

(Hansard, 25.1.66)

While these data show clearly the important role played by British military supplies in keeping the arms race going, exporting arms may equally be argued to help keep the British military industries going. According to SIPRI[6] somewhere between a quarter and a third of military equipment produced is exported. This may help account for the imbalance between the effort put into arms control and into military sales by the British Government.

The Arms Control and Disarmament Office of the Foreign and Comonwealth Office has a staff of 15, of whom six are secretarial and clerical.[10] In contrast the Ministry of Defence's Defence Sales Organisation has over 400 empoyees, while 344 diplomats also engage in military sales promotion.[6]

Britain is by no means the most active arms exporter, but its effort is still hardly designed to reduce global conflict: conflict which is underpinning nuclear proliferation. The British experience demonstrates that while profits are to be made from the Arms Trade, effective measure towards disarmament are unlikely to come from Governments. The opposition to disarmament that will be encountered from firms and people whose jobs depend on the arms trade with possible solutions to this problem are discussed in the section on "conversion" (section 4.1.1.).

2.5 BRITAIN'S MILITARY ROLE

The following paragraphs discuss British military expenditure in detail, showing the part Britain plays in NATO and illustrating how the money is spent. A vast amount of information on military expenditure is available but as the statistics involved are financial, they must be treated carefully. The dangers of international comparisons based on financial data have already been discussed in Section 1. Further difficulties are presented here because of the changing value of the £ so that expenditure in one year can only be compared with that of a later year if adjustment for inflation is made. Although data are comparable within each table, comparison between figures may not be possible.

2.5.1 Britain and NATO

NATO was established in 1949, and took the decision to equip itself with nuclear weapons, now key to its planning, in 1955. NATO currently has 15 members: Spain is negotiating to join, and France co-operates in NATO exercises although De Gaulle took the country out of the military organisation in 1966. Despite its claims to represent the "Free World" NATO encompasses the present military regime in Turkey, and also Greece and Portugal where military governments have held power in recent years.

Figure 2.7 outlines the membership of NATO itself, and that of its Eurogroup which Spain is also planning to join. The Eurogroup spends money over and above national military expenditure. During 1979 the Eurogroup planned to introduce into service: 450 armoured vehicles, 150 artillery pieces, 7500 anti-armour missile and rocket systems, 16 ships and submarines, 400 aircraft and helicopters, and 300 air defence artillery or missile systems.[11]

According to the same source, Eurogroup countries spent over $50 billion on military purposes in 1978. The European countries of NATO contribute 90% of NATO's ground forces, 80% of ships and 75% of aircraft in the European area.[12]

The USA contributes by far the largest share of NATO resources but it is striking that Britain makes an unusually high contribution when viewed in terms of the country's relative economic weakness. In terms of the proportion of national wealth devoted to

Figure 2.7: NATO Members and their military expenditure

		total ($ million)[1]	per capita ($)[1]	as per cent of GDP
	BELGIUM	3700	374	3.3
	DENMARK	1500	297	2.4
	GERMAN FED REP[2]	24400	412	3.3
	GREECE[3]	—	—	—
THE	ITALY	7300	128	2.3
EUROGROUP	LUXEMBOURG[3]	—	—	—
	NETHERLANDS	4900	353	3.3
	NORWAY	1400	356	3.2
	PORTUGAL	800	78	3.8
	TURKEY[3]	—	—	—
	U.K.	19100	340	4.9
	ICELAND	—	—	—
	CANADA	4100	172	1.8
	USA	122300	555	5.2
	FRANCE	22100	413	4.0

1. These figures, which are provisional, have been compiled from NATO sources. The expenditure and per capita figures are based on average market exchange rates for the first 8 months of 1979. These do not necessarily reflect the relative purchasing powers of individual currencies and so are not a complete guide to comparative resource allocation to defence.

2. Germany also incurs expenditure (in the region of $6,400 million in 1979) in support of Berlin. This is not included in the above figure since it falls outside the NATO definition of defence expenditure.

3. Up to date information is not available for Greece, Turkey or Luxembourg. Luxembourg has a very small defence budget, being a very small country. In 1977, Greece and Turkey had expenditures of $1.5 and $2.7 thousand million, respectively (Sivard, 1980).

Source: HMSO, 1980 *Defence in the 1980s – statement on the defence estimates 1980 Vol.1.*

military purposes, this country is behaving more like the USA than other Eurogroup members. For example, for every pound of economic output, Britain spent in 1979 nearly 5p on military activity, while the wealthy Germans spent 3⅓p and the Danes less than half of the U.K amount.

When it comes to nuclear weaponry, Britain is again unique in the Eurogroup. Britain is the only European country to be involved in all three of NATO's strategic nuclear, theatre nuclear and conventional elements; one of the two to provide forces for all three of the major commands (Atlantic, Channel and Europe); and one of the few committing forces to more than one region of Allied Command Europe.

Figure 2.8 indicates Britain's major commitment of forces to NATO. In the event of hostilities, these units would be called into play as part of NATO strategy. It will be noted that nuclear contributions are significant: Britain may not rank with the superpowers in terms of weaponry, but it is important in the alliance's plans for conflict within Europe. Britain's strategic role in part reflects its geographic position, which has made it an important base for U.S forces. Figure 2.9 provides information on these forces and their nuclear weapons. Other forces may be brought in rapidly to augment these in a crisis. Britain is a key base for the U.S military. Not only do we serve as a warehouse for U.S nuclear weapons but U.S intelligence operations (undersea

Figure 2.8: British Forces contributed to NATO, 1978

(1) UK BASE – support for UK forces assigned to NATO. Base facilities for Polaris, for US forces.
(2) EASTERN ATLANTIC AND CHANNEL – UK only W. European nation to operate nuclear-powered attack submarines (10 in service). 17 conventional submarines. Royal Navy virtually all assigned to NATO, and contributes largest part of available naval force. One aircraft carrier, 2 anti-submarine warfare carriers, 23 command helicopter cruisers, 65 destroyers and frigates.
(3) CENTRAL REGION – British Army on the Rhine. 55000 personnel, 600 Chieftain tanks, 2000 other armoured vehicles; tactical nuclear support and RAF support aircraft.
(4) STRATEGIC NUCLEAR FORCES – Polaris (Europe's only nuclear strategic contribution). 192 warheads.
(5) THEATRE NUCLEAR FORCES – in all there are some 7000 tactical nuclear weapons in NATO Europe; UK contributes nuclear capable artillery, aircraft, helicopters and naval forces.
(6) SPECIALIST REINFORCEMENT FORCES – contributes aircraft squadrons, parachute battalions, SAS (Special air-service – 3 squadrons) infantry battalions, commando groups, etc.

Source: mainly from MOD, *NATO – The British Contribution to Allied Defence*, HMSO.

Figure 2.9: NATO in Britain

The U.S. Military Presence in Britain:
(1) Some 27000 personnel (mostly U.S. Air Force), and 31000 dependents.
(2) At least 103 U.S. bases, as against the 56 claimed by the Ministry of Defence.
(3) Nuclear Weapons stored at:
     GLEN DOUGLAS, MACHRINHANISH– submarine weapons, warheads for Poseidon.
     UPPER HEYFORD – F-111 bombers.
     WELFORD – main U.S. storage base, whether nuclear weapons included not certain.
     ALCONBURY, BENTWATERS, LAKENHEATH, WOODBRIDGE – Phantom F4 bombers.
     BURTONWOOD – probably stockpile of 'theatre' nuclear weapons.
(4) Other Functions
     – these include intelligence, communications, general assistance to the U.S. nuclear capability. The U.S. European Command (to be airborne in the case of war) is based at MILDENHALL.
(5) Coming Attractions
     – Cruise missiles are planned for GREENHAM COMMON and MOLESWORTH for 1983.

Source: Duncan Campbell, 'American Bases in Britain' in *Britain and the Bomb. 1981, London: New Statesman.*

surveillance of submarines, spy planes, eavesdropping listening posts to monitor Warsaw Pact communications), the U.S military telephones and computers network, and meteorological information services used in missile targeting are all sited in Britain.

There are two corollaries to Britain's role in NATO, particularly resulting from the close links with the U.S military. First, that military interests in the U.S are unlikely to stand unmoved if Britain seeks not only to abandon the use of weapons of mass destruction, but also refuse to allow British territory to be used for such purposes by others. Second, that while these bases remain Britain remains a prime target for any state engaged in hostilities with the U.S. Because of Britain's key role, it would be surprising if NATO, the beneficiary, did not seek to win public opinion here to its side. Data are, of course, hard to come by but, as an example, Figure 2.10 does manage to bring together some scattered data on NATO propaganda activity within Britain.

NATO propaganda pales to insignificance compared to the public relations activities of the British Military itself. The Ministry of Defence spent around £2 million in TV advertisements in one recent year.[13] Even recruitment campaigns portray particular assumptions about who is the enemy, the glamour of military life, and the existing responsibilities of the wielders of nuclear weapons.

Figure 2.10: NATO Propaganda in Britain

	£
In the period 1976-1980 NATO provided funds to:	
Labour and Trades Union Press Service	32315
British Atlantic Committee: to organise a conference	655
for British Atlantic Youth	6200
The European Atlantic Movement	3000

Additionally NATO supports: The North Atlantic Assembly
(which includes 18 UK parliamentarians out of 172
NATO MPs)
The Atlantic Information Centre for Teachers
(based in London)
Trade Union Atlantic Committee
(based in London)

Sources: *State Research*, 1979, Bulletin No. 10; 1980, Bulletin No. 17.

In 1981 NATO has set up the 'Council for Arms Control', run by luminaries of the above organisations but hoping to obtain wide support from opinion-makers. Details of funding are yet to be announced.
Source: *New Statesman*, 28 August, 1981, *102* (2632).

2.5.2 Britain's Independent Forces

Not all British military activities are directly for the benefit of NATO. Let us firstly briefly consider Britain's own *nuclear* forces, whose "independence" is so often stressed. Britain's "independent" nuclear strategic force is part of the NATO integrated military strategy and forms part of the NATO second strike capability. It is dependent on satellite targetting information supplied by the U.S.

It currently consists of four Polaris submarines, each carrying 16 missiles. They accounted for 1.5% of the military budget in 1980/81, some £165 million; employing 2500 naval and 4500 civilian personnel. More money and labour is consumed in related research and development and communications and other infrastructure e.g docks on which the nuclear force depends must inflate the cost way above these figures.

In the future the Chevaline programme is to add *MIRVs* to Polaris, but since the submarines require replacing within the next decade, the plan to acquire a Trident capability has been developed by subsequent British Governments. Four Trident submarines, each to be equiped with 16 missiles – the destructive power of a thousand Hiroshimas – will be acquired, at the cost of (at a conservative estimate) well over £1.5 billion each, if these plans are not reversed.[14] In fact the projected cost of Trident is continually escalating. An article in the Financial Times[15] suggests that the real cost of the Trident programme is likely to be in the order of £9 billion.

Britain's nuclear force appears to account in itself for a relatively small percentage of the country's overall military budget (figure 2.11); however, many support and other services will be dedicated to, or used extensively to form part of the nuclear system.

Because of its colonial legacy Britain, unlike most European NATO countries, still retains a considerable military presence outside the NATO area, which underlies a significant proportion of the expenditure shown in figure 2.12.

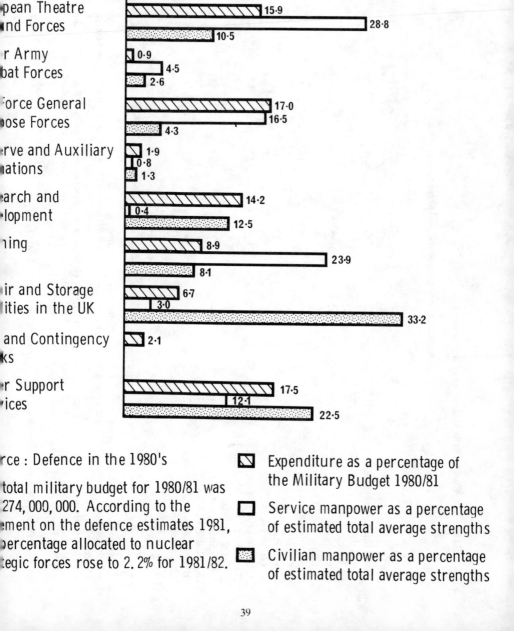

ear Strategic
e
- 1·5
- 0·8
- 1·8

l General Purpose
bat Forces
- 13·4
- 9·2
- 3·2

pean Theatre
nd Forces
- 15·9
- 28·8
- 10·5

r Army
bat Forces
- 0·9
- 4·5
- 2·6

orce General
ose Forces
- 17·0
- 16·5
- 4·3

rve and Auxiliary
ations
- 1·9
- 0·8
- 1·3

arch and
lopment
- 14·2
- 0·4
- 12·5

ing
- 8·9
- 23·9
- 8·1

ir and Storage
ities in the UK
- 6·7
- 3·0
- 33·2

and Contingency
ks
- 2·1

r Support
ices
- 17·5
- 12·1
- 22·5

rce : Defence in the 1980's

total military budget for 1980/81 was
274,000,000. According to the
ment on the defence estimates 1981,
ercentage allocated to nuclear
egic forces rose to 2.2% for 1981/82.

▨ Expenditure as a percentage of
the Military Budget 1980/81

☐ Service manpower as a percentage
of estimated total average strengths

▦ Civilian manpower as a percentage
of estimated total average strengths

Figure 2.12: The Cost of British Overseas Engagement

Defence balance of payments: invisible transactions

	Outturn[1]				Estimate[1]	
	1975-1976	1976-77	1977-78	1978-79	1979-80	1980-81
TOTAL DEBITS	726	815	811	832	997	1215
Total military services	712	796	789	809	966	1187
Local defence expenditure	585	670	673	769	813	935
of which:						
Germany	405	513	527	619	661	763
Other NATO areas	30	34	39	41	49	49
Mediterranean	66	68	70	77	67	80
Gulf	4	3	1	1	1	1
Far East	60	33	17	10	12	14
Other areas	20	19	19	21	23	28
Other military services[2]	127	126	116	125	153	252
Transfers – contributions to international defence organisations	14	19	22	23	31	28
TOTAL CREDITS	74	64	78	166	130	113
Receipts from US forces	24	28	47	51	66	70
Other receipts[3]	50	36	31	115	64	43
NET BALANCE (– = debit)	–652	–751	–733	–751	–867	–1102

1. Outturn and Estimates are given at outturn and Estimates prices respectively.
2. Including contributions to infrastucture projects (net) and payments for R&D levies. Receipts for R&D levies, etc., are entered as "other receipts".
3. Includes offset receipts from the Federal Republic of Germany (Exchange of Notes between the Government of the United Kingdom of Great Britain and Northern Ireland and the Government of the Federal Republic of Germany for offsetting the Foreign Exchange Expenditure on British Forces in the Federal Republic of Germany: Cmnd. 6970).

Source: HMSO, *Defence in the 1980s*, vol. 2 (Defence Statistics) 1980 HMSO.

2.5.3 Britain's Military Expenditure

Spending on the military is, as we have seen in figure 2.7, a relatively favoured activity in this country. Figure 2.13 compares military expenditure to other government expenditure showing that in 1980, military expenditure was comparable to that for education, or the National Health Service. While only about one-tenth of all central government expenditure, military spending is clearly a factor of considerable significance when arguments are raised about the need to cut education and health services.

In general, the greatest proportion of military expenditure goes on equipment together with building, stores, etc. This accounts for 60% of costs while pay and pensions consume the rest.[16]

The information shown here suggests that, compared to other European countries, Britain is spending a disproportionate share of her income on the military. Also, as a substantial proportion of the expense occurs overseas, military activity contributes a net deficit to our balance of payments that is even larger than the profits received from the arms trade.

Figure 2.13: **Military and Social Expenditure, UK**

£ Thousand Millions at current prices

	1975	1977	1979	1980
General government total expenditure				
of: Military	5.2	6.9	9.0	11.4
NHS	5.1	6.8	8.8	11.5
Education	6.6	7.8	9.6	11.9
Social Security	8.9	13.2	18.5	22.2
Housing	4.5	5.1	6.1	7.2
Debt Interest	4.2	6.4	9.0	11.3
Other	17.1	15.7	23.9	28.2
TOTAL	51.6	61.9	84.9	103.7

Source: Central Statistical Office – *National Income and Expenditure* 1981 edition, London: HMSO.

UK-based MOD contractors paid £5 million or more by MOD for equipment 1979/80

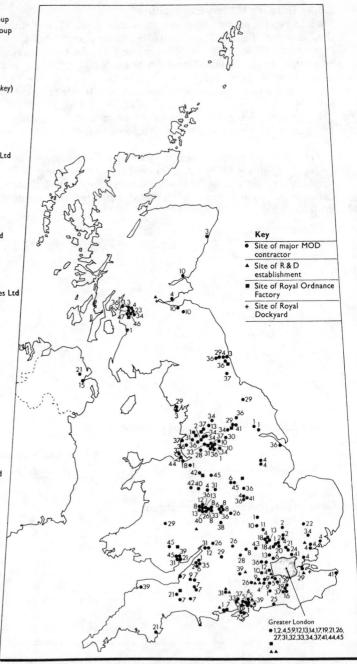

Over £100m
1   British Aerospace Aircraft Group
2   British Aerospace Dynamic Group
3   British Shipbuilders
4   The General Electric Co Ltd
5   The Plessey Co Ltd
6   Rolls-Royce Ltd
    Royal Ordnance Factories (see key)
7   Westland Aircraft Ltd

£50m–£100m
8   BL Ltd
9   EMI Ltd
10 Ferranti Ltd
11 Hunting Associated Industries Ltd

£25m–£50m
12 Dowty Group Ltd
13 Lucas Industries Ltd
14 Racal Electronics Ltd
15 Short Bros. Ltd

£10m–£25m
16 British Electric Traction Co Ltd
17 Decca Ltd
18 Vauxhall Motors Ltd
19 Gresham Lion Ltd
20 Hawker Siddeley Group Ltd
21 Standard Telephones and Cables Ltd
22 Marshall of Cambridge
    (Engineering) Ltd
23 Pilkington Bros. Ltd
24 Cossor Electronics Ltd
25 The Singer Co (UK) Ltd
26 Smiths Industries Ltd
27 Thorn Electrical Industries Ltd
28 UK Atomic Energy Authority
29 Vickers Ltd

£5m–£10m
30 David Brown Holdings Ltd
31 BTR Ltd
32 Cable and Wireless Ltd
33 Chloride Group Ltd
34 Courtaulds Ltd
35 Dickinson Robinson Group Ltd
36 Dunlop Holdings Ltd
37 Philips Electronic &
    Associated Industries Ltd
38 Ford Motor Co Ltd
39 Grindlays Holdings Ltd
40 Guest Keen & Nettlefolds Ltd
41 Rank Organisation Ltd
42 Rolls-Royce Motor
    Holdings Ltd.
43 Ropner Holdings Ltd
44 Stone Platt Industries Ltd
45 Vantona Group Ltd
46 Weir Group Ltd
47 Yarrow & Co Ltd

Key
● Site of major MOD contractor
▲ Site of R & D establishment
■ Site of Royal Ordnance Factory
+ Site of Royal Dockyard

Greater London
● 1,2,4,5,9,12,13,14,17,19,21,26, 27,31,32,33,34,37,41,44,45

Source: *Statement on the defence estimates 1981*, Vol 1.

2.6 MILITARY PRODUCTION

We have already noted some of the beneficiaries of the arms trade. But what firms are involved in military production for the British military system? And what is their role in nuclear production?

Figure 2.14 identifies major military contractors in the U.K. In 1979/80 there were nearly 50 firms receiving more than £5 million for their Ministry of Defence sales, of whom 11 received at least ten times this figure. And at a time when many other firms are feeling the pinch, it is obvious that military producers are in an exceptionally favoured position, as figure 2.15 demonstrates. These big contractors generally show a very healthy ratio of profits to sales. And the outlook is for more of the same: the 1981 Defence Review, generally heralded as meaning 'cuts', added over 1.5 billion of orders for aircraft and missiles for the 1980's to a backlog of orders for aircraft of some £6 billion (figure 2.16).

**Figure 2.15: Major Arms Companies;
Sales and Profits**

	Total Sales[1]	Pre-Tax Profits	Latest Year	Approximate Value of 1980 MOD Contracts
GEC - Marconi (Avionics/ Electronics)	£3005.8m	£415.7m	March 1980	Over £100m
Thorn - EMI (Avionics/ Electronics)	£1620.9m	£125.5m	March 1980	Over £ 50m
Lucas (Aerospace/ Hydraulics)	£1195.9m	£ 39.1m	July 1980	Between £25-50m
British Aerospace	£1027.4m	£ 44.4m	Dec 1977	Over £100m
Plessey (Avionics/ Electronics)	£ 751.0m	£ 60.1m	March 1980	Over £100m
Rank Organisation	£ 596.7m	£111.2m	Oct 1980	Between £5-10m
Vickers (Engineering)	£ 389.8m	£ 7.3m	Dec 1979	Between £10-25m
Smiths Industries (Avionics/ Electronics)	£ 319.8m	£ 26.1m	Aug 1980	Between £10-25m
Racal (Avionics/ Electronics)	£ 263.7m	£ 63.6m	March 1980	Between £25-50m
Ferranti (Avionics/ Electronics	£ 214.6m	£ 11.2	March 1980	Between £50-100m

1. Includes non-military products.

Source: *MOD Defence Estimates 1981* and *Labour Research*

Figure 2.16: New Military Orders in 1981 Defence Review

	Estimated cost	Principle companies Benefitting
A V-88 Harrier	£1bn plus*	British Aerospace (military aircraft division)
Improved Pegasus engine for Harrier	(included in above)	Rolls-Royce Bristol
Tracked Rapier anti-aircraft missiles	£160m	BAe Dynamics Group
Sea Skua helicopter-borne missile	£200m[1]	BAe Dynamics Group
Sea Eagle anti-ship missile	[3]	BAe Dynamics Group
EH-101 anti-submarine helicopter	£20m[2]	Westland Helicopters
VC-10 tanker modifications	£131m	BAe Civil Aircraft Division
IP-233 anti-airfield weapon	[3]	Hunting Engineering
Blowpipe missile improvements	[3]	Short Brothers

* The estimated value of work going to the UK. The cost of the UK of its own 60 aircraft would be much less and is not disclosed.
1. Total development and initial production costs.
2. Initial contract only.
3. Costs not disclosed.

Source: *Financial Times,* 8 July 1981, p.21

The biggest involvement is with British Aerospace, from whom other firms subcontract as well as making deals direct with the Ministry. British Aerospace is currently developing the Tornado, one model of which – the Interdictor Strike Tornado, costing over £11 million each – is nuclear capable. There is speculation that it may be equipped with cruise missiles. Nearly 400 Tornados are to be purchased by the MOD, costing over £5 billion. The current nuclear-capable squadrons of the RAF amount to over 200 aircraft – all manufactured by British Aerospace.

Nuclear weapons production itself is rather too sensitive to be entrusted to private hands. The Atomic Weapons Research Establishment at Aldermaston (near Reading), is largely responsible for R & D and manufacture of these weapons; other factories are at Burghfield and Cardiff. Aldermaston employs 5 000 people and costs £100 millions per annum: it was here that the Chevaline missile was developed. Although Trident missiles are to be bought from the USA (Lockheed) at a cost of £18-25 millions (excluding warhead, which will be manufactured locally), Trident submarines will probably be built in British shipyards at some £500 millions each.

It is obvious enough that some sectors of industry profit from weapons production – and that the large and the relatively secure profits that are found here lead to a diversion of effort into these sectors. It is argued that this is at least beneficial in that jobs are created. Obviously money used in other more productive ways (in the sense of creating wealth for the future) can create far more jobs, bcause military production is relatively capital-intensive.

It is possible to indicate how important military expenditure is to different industrial sectors. Aerospace equipment manufacturers are the single biggest beneficiaries, as we already know, followed by radar and electronic capital goods, shipbuilding, and the oil industry. This does not show how important military expenditure is to each industry, however. Nearly half of aerospace equipment, ⅓ of shipbuilding output involved the military.[17] (These figures were obtained by dividing Military purchases by total output: the figures are higher if net output is taken). Other industries had much lower military intensities, with only electronics and telecommunications exceeding 1/10 and most others following well below this. Conversion, then, has to begin with these industries which are very 'high' technology oriented: case studies for such industries are described in Section 4.1.1.

2.7 MILITARY RESEARCH

As well as pushing the *economy* in a particular direction, the role of the military in our society affects *scientific research*. About half the R & D funded by the government is carried out for military purposes, as figure 2.17 shows.[18] It is likely that the expenditure on 'space' and 'industrial' R & D includes military-related work: even 'social and sociological problems' encompasses counter-insurgency research. Further, given that 23 300 civilians in the Department of Environment, and 2 900 in meteorological services, are employed directly on military work,[19] we may have our suspicions about categories like 'exploration of the Earth and its environment'. Given that much industrial R & D is carried out in aerospace and electronics, it is likely that a sizeable proportion of private R & D, too, is directed toward military aims.

Figure 2.17:   British State Expenditure on R and D by Sector, 1977/78

Sector	£ million	% of total R&D budget
Exploration and exploitation of and its environment	16.9	1.03
Planning of the human environment	32.0	1.94
Health	45.9	2.79
Energy	112.4	6.82
Agriculture	75.6	4.59
Industry	88.5	5.37
Social and sociological problems	17.8	1.08
Space	43.3	2.63
Military	862.8	52.38
General promotion of knowledge	352.0	21.37
TOTAL	£1647.2	100%

Source: CSO, *Annual Abstract of Statistics, 1980,* London: HMSO.

Indeed, the heavy weighting of the military's concerns in scientific work makes it likely that the whole process of deciding what problems are important to research, and how they can best be studied, is influenced by criteria developed by the military. For example, many researchers trained in space research (e.g radio astronomy) go on to careers working with radar and missile systems. This is made possible because the same sorts of technology have come to be developed in "pure" and military-applied science.

We do not know how many people are directly involved in military R & D, but the *Statement on the Defence Estimates 1981*,[19] suggests that in 1981/82 around 32 thousand workers will be employed by the Ministry of Defence on military R & D at a cost of £1676 million (meteorological R & D is not included in these figures).

Figure 2.18 using data from the same source, provides a breakdown of the in-house and contracted-out R & D. The distribution of money between universities and private industry and other bases has been pretty constant over recent years.

Figure 2.18: **Distribution of Military R and D Expenditure**

£ million

	1976-77	1981-82 (est)
Total expenditure[1]	713	1738
Intra-mural R and D	279	517
Extra-mural: private industry (and public companies)	433	1088
Universities and other further education	3	6
Other votes and central government funds	9	12
Overseas	67	104
Other	—	10

1. This includes Social Science R&D, not covered in the detailed breakdown: amounting to £1 million in 1976-77 and 1981-82 alike.

Source: *Statement on the Defence Estimates, 1981*, Vol. 2. London: HMSO

There are 34 Ministry of Defence research establishments, but these have experienced problems in recruiting appropriate personnel. Therefore a push for more involvement with educational establishments has been developed. The current Chief Scientist at the Ministry has set up a series of defence seminars in which the MOD's interests and the academic's abilities are compared – these are the places in which contracts are first dreamed up. Careers of mutual concern are being identified with the Science and Engineering Research Council and with military research under less financial pressure than other research, its role in higher education is increasing. Topics of interest include: surveillance, applied psychology, artificial intelligence and space research.[20]

Some £6 million from the Ministry of Defence is given to research in higher education establishments in Britain. Up-to-date information on the number of projects that are involved is still being produced: but in 1974 there were six hundred such projects.[21] A parliamentary answer to Frank Allaun on 12 March 1981 stated that there are more typically around 500 research agreements between the MOD and universities and polytechnics, with a typical length of 3 years. It is claimed that little of this research is classified, but details were refused of this, and of whether investigators are subjected, to security clearance etc. Recent, as yet unpublished, CND research suggests that US Defence Department funding has more than doubled since Fairbairn's analysis. NATO also provides research fellowships, and is well known as a lavish provider of funds to attend its meetings and seminars. The Ministry of Defence also funds defence lectureships at selected universities.[16]

There is little definite that can be said about military scientific efforts in the world as a whole, though an estimate of ½ million world wide working on military R & D has been made.[22] In the light of the British data this seems a surprisingly low figure, even if we accept that British science is more militarised than that in most other countries. Gutteridge puts the amount spent on military research worldwide as $25 billion (more than four times that spent on medical research).[22]

2.8 CONCLUSIONS

It should be abundantly clear that our economy – and through education and research, our technology and even our thinking – have been considerably moulded around the military. The short term interests that this generates, from affected researchers and soldiers through to their political representatives – and not forgetting the recipients of the profits of the military industries – must constitute a powerful opposition that must be overcome in order to achieve disarmament.

References

1. Nield R. *How to make up your mind about the bomb.* London: Andre Deutsch 1981.
2. *Long term world wide effects of multiple nuclear weapons detonations.* Washington DC: National Academy of Sciences 1975.
3. Blackaby F. *A million dollars a minute for the military. Guardian* May 21 1980. See also The nuclear arms race *Peace Studies Paper No 4.* School of Peace Studies, University of Bradford 1981.
4. Sivard R. *World handbook of military and social expenditures.* Laedsburg Va: World Priorities 1980.
5. Smith D. *South Africa's nuclear capability.* London: World Campaign Against Military and Nuclear collaboration with South Africa 1980.
6. Stockholm International Peace Research Institute. *SIPRI yearbook 1980.*
7. Rogers P, Dando M, Van der Dungen P. *As lambs to the slaughter.* London: Arrow 1980.
8. Kidron M, Segal R. *The state of the world atlas.* London: Pan 1981.
9. ACDA. *World military expenditure and arms transfers.* Washington: Government Printing Office 1980.

10. *ADIU Report. 3(1)*. Brighton 1981.
11. NATO. *NATO Handbook*. Brussels: NATO Information Service. May 1979.
12. Ministry of Defence. *NATO – The British contribution to allied defence*. London: HMSO 1979.
13. *ADIU Report. 2(3)*. Brighton 1980.
14. Smith D. *The defence of the realm in the 1980s*. London: Croom Helm 1980.
15. Bloom B. A time bomb under Trident. *Financial Times*. November 2 1981.
16. *Defence in the 1980s. Statement on the defence estimates. Vol 1*. Cmnd 7826-1. London: HMSO 1980.
17. Central Statistical Office. *Input-Output Tables 1968*. Studies in official statistics. No. 22. London: HMSO 1973.
18. *ADIU Report. 1(3)*. Brighton 1979.
19. *Defence in the 1980s. Statement on the defence estimates. Vol. 2*. Cmnd 7826-II. London: HMSO 1980. (Table 5.2)
20. Redfearn J. New customers. *Nature 1980; 285: 526* (June 19)
21. Fairbairns Z. *Study war no more*. London: CND 1974.
22. Gutteridge W. in *ADIU Report 1(3)*. Brighton 1979.

3 THE EFFECTS OF NUCLEAR WAR

"Hiroshima does not look like a bombed city. It looks as if a monster steamroller has passed over it and squashed it out of existence. I write these facts as dispassionately as I can in the hope that they will act as a warning to the world."

Daily Express, September 5, 1945

The reporter who wrote these words went on to describe the destruction he saw, commenting that it was on a much larger scale than anything he had seen in four years of World War II. The nuclear attacks being planned today are another order of magnitude larger still, both in terms of the sizes of the weapons and also of the numbers of weapons it is intended to use.

The question "What would be the effects of a nuclear attack on Britain?" is virtually unanswerable. To start with, we do not know where the weapons are due to explode, whether they would hit targets, or what size they would be. Even if this was known, it would still not be possible to estimate their overall effects. The physical effects of nuclear explosions can be estimated using data derived from nuclear tests carried out in the past. These were, however, done in uninhabited areas, many of them at sea. These mean that it is not clear to what extent the results are applicable to inhabited areas and the very variable British weather conditions. The effects on human beings and plant life can be estimated using the experiences of Hiroshima and Nagasaki, although the bombs exploded there were relatively small compared with modern weapons. In addition, the extent of the damage made it impossible to know exactly how many people perished in the explosions at Hiroshima and Nagasaki. While survey teams from other parts of Japan arrived fairly soon after the attacks to try to quantify their effects, it was not until some months later that systematic records of deaths came to be kept again.[1] This means that data from these cities must be used with caution. What could not, in any case, be extrapolated from the nuclear attacks on these two Japanese cities, is the total effect on a country and its infrastructure of a large number of such attacks.

Data have however been derived to enable some sort of assessment of the likely outcome of a set of attacks under given conditions. It is clear that the Government is making use of the results of this sort of calculation.[2] Lord Belstead, formerly the minister responsible for civil defence said that while "only fifteen million" British people would survive a full scale nuclear war, the figure could be doubled if people followed the instructions they were given.[3] Put another way, this means that 24 million would die, even in the latter case. John Clayton, Director of the Home Office Scientific Advisory Branch, has been reported as saying that a nuclear attack on the United Kingdom equivalent to 3000 megatons (considerably more than is usually suggested) would leave just 10 million of the population alive afterwards.[4] The Home Office, in its guide *Domestic Nuclear Shelters*[5] quotes an estimate that in the event of a nuclear attack equivalent to 200 megatons on the United Kingdom, "about 80 percent of the land might suffer no blast effect at all."

In this section, we describe how these sorts of estimates are made and point out why they produce inconsistencies. Despite these, and other deficiencies, we think that the data we present are useful in illustrating the magnitude of the effects. Because of this, we also describe how local groups can use the data to build a picture of the effects of a one megaton attack on a target in their area. We have chosen one megaton because many warheads of this size exist, but they are by no means the largest.

While it is difficult enough to assess the immediate effects of a nuclear attack, it is virtually impossible to predict what might befall the survivors. Government publications such as *Domestic nuclear shelters*[5] are relatively silent on this and concentrate almost exclusively on measures which, they claim, would enable people to survive the first fortnight after an attack. While we do not attempt to present data on the aftermath, we outline why we think that many of those who survived the first fortnight after an attack would be at very high risk of dying at a later stage.

Units of measurement
As the data presented in this section have been derived over a period of years using a variety of units of measurement, we have used the units in the original texts, rather than attempt to convert to the internationally agreed SI units. For those who wish to do so, we list conversion factors below.

Original unit	SI unit
1 mile	1.609 kilometres
1 pound per square inch (psi)	6895 Newtons per square metre
	.006895 megapascals (Mpa)
1 rad	.01 Gray
1 rem	.01 Sievert
1 calorie	4.187 Joules
1000 megawatts	1 gigawatt (electrical) (GW(e))

3.1   WHAT ARE THE IMMEDIATE EFFECTS OF A NUCLEAR EXPLOSION?

The description given here is only a brief summary of more detailed accounts available elsewhere.[6][7][8][9] These, in their turn, rely heavily on a more technical book, *The effects of nuclear weapons*,[10] from which many of the data which we present are also derived. A Japanese book *Hiroshima and Nagasaki* which is now available in English[1] brings together photographs, data and descriptions of the personal experiences of survivors of the attacks on Hiroshima and Nagasaki. A particular point to note in these accounts is that while British civil defence plans seem to assume a sort of "Dunkerque spirit", the victims in Japan did not react in this way.[1][11]

3.1.1   Blast
The blast of a nuclear explosion produces two types of damaging effect. The first is sudden increases in air pressure which are strong enough to crush objects. This is called "static overpressure" and is measured as the amount by which the air pressure exceeds the normal air pressure of 14.7 pounds per square inch (psi) at sea level. The "peak overpressure", or maximum value, occurs when the blast wave arrives. The other effect, known as "dynamic pressure" takes the form of high winds which can move objects and knock them down. People and objects such as trees and telegraph poles would be likely

50

to be blown down by the wind while buildings would be destroyed by the overpressure.

The extent of the blast damage depends both on the power of the bomb and the height above the ground at which it explodes. Exploding a bomb at ground level would maximise the overpressure at very close ranges so these "surface bursts" would be used to attack very hard targets such as missile silos. An "air burst", on the other hand, would not produce such high overpressures underneath the explosion, but would spread the effects of the blast over a wider area. Figure 3.1 shows the distances from "ground zero" (the point on the ground directly below the centre of the explosion) at which given overpressures would be experienced if a one megaton bomb were exploded at an altitude of 8000 feet or at ground level. Figure 3.2 shows the likely effects of various ranges of overpressures on buildings.

Relatively few people would die of the direct effects of blast as overpressures of up to 30 p.s.i. are not lethal on their own. Overpressures of up to 5 p.s.i. can, however, rupture eardrums. Blast effects would kill many people indirectly as a result of being caught in collapsing buildings or being struck by falling or flying objects. It is difficult to assess what proportion of the population would be affected by a given overpressure. The estimates shown in Figure 3.1 were made by the US Office of Technology Assessment, which described them as "relatively conservative".[8] They would appear to apply to urban areas.

The Home Office's estimates appear to be rather lower than this,[2] but direct comparisons are difficult as it uses different cut off points from the Office of Technology Assessment. The Home Office defines an "A ring" in which overpressures are 11 psi or more. Within this ring it estimates that the fatality level could exceed 85 percent without blast shelter protection. It defines a "B ring" within which overpressures are at least 6, but under 11 psi, and it estimates that at least 40 percent of people in this area would die unless protected by blast shelters. In the "C ring" (from 1.5 to 6 psi) it says that "blast could cause lethal flying missiles." There is no mention of blast fatalities in the "D ring" (from .75 to 1.5 psi).

3.1.2 Heat and light

About 35 percent of the energy from a nuclear explosion is an intense burst of light and heat (thermal radiation), the duration of which depends on the power of the explosion. This heat flash travels at 186000 miles per second and therefore will reach people before the blast wave. Anyone who is looking in the direction of the explosion will suffer temporary blindness which can last for several minutes. It could well prevent them from being able to take steps to avoid the effects of the blast wave. A one megaton explosion can cause temporary blindess as far away as 13 miles on a clear day or 53 miles on a clear night.

The more intense heat found closer to the site of the explosion can cause skin burns. A one megaton explosion is capable of causing first degree burns (equivalent to bad sunburn) at distances of about seven miles, second degree burns (producing blisters which may lead to infection, if left untreated, and are likely to leave permanent scars) at about six miles and third degree burns (which destroy tissue) at about five miles. A person with third degree burns over 24 percent of the body or second degree burns over 30 percent of the body will suffer from severe shock and will probably die unless medical treatment is available.

It is difficult to estimate the numbers of people who would sustain burns in a major attack on an urban centre. The variable factors include the number of people in the open at the time of the attack, the clothing worn and skin colour – dark clothing and skin absorb more light and heat than do light ones. Other factors are the height of the

Figure 3.1 Blast and burn effects on people of a 1 megaton bomb

(i) Injuries from blast and heat

Peak overpressure psi	Deaths and injuries from blast % killed	% injured	% uninjured	Burns in unprotected survivors Explosion at 8000 feet	Explosion at ground level
12 and over	98[1]	2	0	Nearly all would have 3rd degree burns	Nearly all would have 3rd degree burns
5-11	50	40	10		
2-4	5	45	50	2nd and 3rd burns	
1	0	25	75	1st and 2nd degree burns	1st, 2nd and some 3rd degree burns

1 If the explosion was at ground level, everyone in this area would be killed.

(ii) Extent of blast at various distances from ground zero of a 1 megaton explosion

Peak overpressure psi	Distance from ground zero, miles Explosion at 8000 feet	Explosion at ground level[2]
100	–	1.0
20	1.3	2.1
12	3.7	2.7
10	4.8	3.2
5	7.1	4.3
3	9.5	6.1
2	12.6	7.6
1	18.7	11.9

2 An explosion at ground level would leave a crater at ground zero at least 175 feet deep and 700 feet in diameter.
Source: Estimated from *The effects of nuclear war*[8] and *The effects of nuclear weapons*[10].

Figure 3.2: Some effects of blast from explosion of a 1 Megaton weapon

Distance from ground zero, miles		Peak over-pressure psi	Peak wind velocity mph	Typical effects of blast
Surface explosion	Explosion at 8000ft			
1.3	.8	20	470	Reinforced concrete structures are levelled.
2.0	3.0	10	290	Most factories and small commercial buildings collapse.
2.7	4.4	5	160	Lightly constructed commercial buildings and private houses are destroyed. Heavier construction is severely damaged.
3.8	5.9	3	95	Walls of typical steel frame buildings and private houses are destroyed. Heavier construction is severely damaged.
7.4	11.6	1	35	Damage to some structures. People endangered by flying glass and debris.

Source: *The effects of nuclear war*[8]

Figure 3.3: Some effects of heat from explosion of a 1 Megaton weapon

Distance from ground zero, miles		Thermal radiation cal/cm²	Effects of thermal radiation
Surface explosion	Explosion at 8000ft		
4.0	4.5	20	Dark furnishing fabrics catch fire
4.5	5.0	18	Dark coloured cotton catches fire
4.7	5.6	15	Unpainted wood chars
5.0	6.1	13	All unprotected skin would have third degree burns
5.4	6.9	10	About half the unprotected people would have third degree burns
5.8	7.5	8	Newspaper catches fire
6.5	8.6	6	About half the unprotected people would have second degree burns
8.0	11.5	3	About half the unprotected people would have first degree burns

Estimated from data in *The effects of nuclear weapons*[10]

explosion (an air burst spreads thermal radiation further away than a ground burst) and weather conditions. Smog and moisture tend to absorb thermal radiation. Figures 3.1 and 3.3 give estimates of burn injuries and other effects which could result from being exposed to the heat from a one megaton bomb exploded when the visibility is 12 miles. This is not unusual in urban areas on a clear day.

In addition to burns caused directly by the heat of the explosion, further burns can result from the fires which this heat can cause. It has been estimated that about ten percent of all buildings exposed to blast pressures of five psi and two percent of those exposed to blast pressures of two psi would also have serious fires. There have been suggestions that when the blast wave arrived, it would help to put out fires, but the evidence is inconclusive. Indeed there is a possibility that the winds might cause individual fires to coalesce into fire storms as happened at Hiroshima. It is rather more certain that any surviving fire brigades would have difficulty in reaching and fighting fires because the roads would be blocked by debris.

3.1.3 Radiation

There are two ways in which nuclear radiation can affect people, animals and plants. Initial radiation (also called "direct" or "prompt" radiation) is emitted at the time of the explosion. While it can be very intense, its range is limited. So although it did considerable damage to the people of Hiroshima and Nagasaki, the range of direct radiation from the much larger weapons being stockpiled today is less than the range of the lethal effects of blast and heat.

The exception to this is the neutron bomb or "enhanced radiation warhead", to give it its more correct name. The aim of those designing it is to make a warhead which will release the maximum amount of energy in the form of initial radiation and the minimum as blast and heat so as to destroy life rather than property. At present though, these warheads release only 30-40 percent of their energy as radiation. As the typical neutron warhead has a yield of around one kiloton, the resulting blast and heat effects are far from negligible.[12]

Measures of radiation

Several different units are used as measures of radiation. The Roentgen (sometimes abbreviated to r) is a measure of energy. It describes the amount of ionisation produced when radiation is absorbed in air (one Roentgen produces 2.58×10^{-4} Coulombs kg^{-1} in air for either positive or negative ions). The rad is a measure of the amount of energy absorbed per unit mass (one rad is an absorption of 10×10^{-3} Joules kg^{-1}). Materials differ in their ability to absorb radiation. Human body tissue absorbs approximately one rad when exposed to one Roentgen of radiation. Some forms of radiation have more damaging effects on human tissue than others. The rem (Roentgen equivalent man) is defined as the amount of radiation required to cause a particular amount of body damage. One Roentgen of gamma rays will cause an absorbed dose of approximately one rem in human tissue. This means that the three units, the Roentgen, the rad and the rem can be taken as being roughly equivalent to each other for the purpose of calculating the effects of the radiation damage caused to humans by a nuclear attack.

The second way radiation can spread is through fallout. If a bomb exploded high enough above ground level not to make a crater, there would not be very much fallout. Even so, the relatively low doses of radiation emitted are of the type which would be easily absorbed in the human body. For example strontium-90 would be absorbed in human bones.

If a nuclear weapon exploded on or near the Earth's surface, it would make a crater and pulverised earth, stones, dust and other material would be sucked up into the fireball and become radioactive as a result of being bombarded by neutrons. The heaviest particles would spill out again around the site of the explosion. The lighter particles would rise higher and be carried some distance downwind before returning to the ground as radioactive fallout. This means that fallout travels much more slowly than the blast wave. The fallout during the period of approximately one day after an explosion consists largely of dust and isotopes emitting mainly gamma rays, and to a lesser extent, beta rays. Fallout continues long after this, however, but it is likely to take the form of radioactive isotopes such as cesium-137, strontium-90 and carbon-14 in food and water.

Figure 3.4 illustrates how, theoretically, the fallout from a one megaton bomb exploding at ground level would be distributed if the wind blew steadily at 15 mph. It is expressed in terms of the radiation emitted in the first 24 hours after the explosion. In practice, both changes in wind speed and direction, and the interaction between the effects of multiple bomb bursts over a small area, would be likely to cause considerable local variations in this pattern.

Figure 3.4: Fallout from a 1 megaton surface explosion, assuming 50% of energy of explosion derived from fission

Accumulated dose at 24 hours rads	Downwind distance miles	Maximum width miles	Ground zero width miles
5000	19	2.4	1.1
2000	26	4.5	2.3
1000	36	6.1	3.2
600	49	7.6	3.9
450	60	8.4	4.3
200	95	11.8	5.4
100	144	17.5	6.3

Estimated from data in *The effects of nuclear weapons*[10]

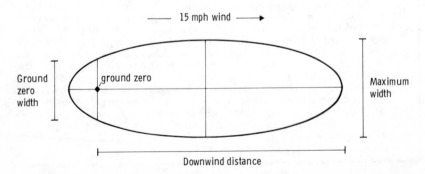

The effects of acute exposure to radiation on people are summarised below. Acute exposure is usually taken, in this context, as being exposure over a 24 hour period. The effects are discussed in detail in Joseph Rotblat's book *Nuclear radiation in warfare*.[13]

(i) At very high doses (which Rotblat estimates as being 2000 rads and above), people exposed would be disorientated and incapacitated immediately. This is because radiation would directly affect their central nervous systems, resulting in convulsions, lack of muscular coordination, coma and shock. Most of those exposed would die in two or three hours. It is intended that neutron warheads will give radiation doses of this magnitude.

(ii) At slightly lower doses (Rotblat quotes 500-2000 rads), the lining of the small intestine and bowel is destroyed. This results first in diarrhoea and vomiting, which leads on to diarrhoea with blood in the stools and thence to dehydration, followed by death in a week to ten days. There is also damage to the bone marrow, but it is overshadowed by the damage to the gut.

(iii) At still lower levels (Rotblat suggests 100-500 rads), the gut is less affected, but death can result from damage to the bone marrow. This damage leads to bleeding, bruising and vulnerability to infection and can cause death within two or three weeks. Even if the exposed person survives beyond that time, bone marrow failure or infection can still cause death during the next year or two. Those who survive as long as the third week after exposure are likely to lose their hair.

(iv) People exposed to radiation doses at the bottom end of this range, say around 100 rads, would have a relatively low risk of dying, but would probably experience at least some of the symptoms of radiation sickness, which is more correctly described as the prodomal syndrome. The symptoms can include anorexia, nausea, vomiting, diarrhoea, intestinal cramps, dehydration, fatigue, apathy or listlessness, fever and headache. Only if a person is exposed to a high dose of radiation, will all the symptoms occur, and they will not all be present during the first 48 hours after exposure. Figure 3.5 indicates doses at which some of these symptoms can occur.

Figure 3.5:   Radiation doses in rads which produce early radiation sickness symptoms

Percentage of exposed population suffering from symptom

Symptom	10%	50%	90%
Anorexia	0.4	1.0	2.4
Nausea	0.5	1.7	3.2
Vomiting	0.6	2.1	3.8
Diarrhoea	0.9	2.4	3.9

Source: *Radiobiological factors in manned space flight*[14] Quoted in *Nuclear radiation in warfare*[13]

The LD50, which is the dose which is likely to kill 50 percent of those receiving it, is 450 rads for acute exposures. A given dose of radiation absorbed in a short time is, however, more harmful than the same dose absorbed over a longer period. The LD50 is 600 rads for doses accumulated over a fortnight, and 650 rads for doses accumulated over a month. The LD100, that is the dose which no one is likely to survive is 600 rads for acute exposures. All these estimates assume that the person is receiving treatment (antibiotics, blood transfusions etc), something which is unlikely to occur after a nuclear attack. Indeed, *The effects of nuclear weapons*,[10] goes as far as to suggest that people exposed to 600 and 1000 rads have some hope of surviving and suggests the possibility of a bone marrow transplant. This technique is still considered to be experimental even when full medical facilities are available!

There are also a number of after effects of exposure to nuclear radiation which do not appear until some time later. People exposed have an increased risk of developing cataracts, leukaemia and certain types of cancer, notably cancer of the thyroid, the lung and bones, and, in women, the breast.[13] The incidence of cancer including leukaemia in those exposed to low level radiation has been estimated as 100/million persons/rad.[14] In other words, if a million people were exposed to a dose of 100 rads, it would be expected that 10000 of them would develop cancer. The corresponding rate for leukaemia alone is 15 to 25 cases/million persons/rad and for childhood cancers after being exposed as a fetus is 200 to 250/million persons/rad.[14]

These estimates are far from precise as they depend on the form of the mathematical relationship which is assumed between the dose and the response.[14] The data used include data from Hiroshima and Nagasaki as well as data derived from various other sources including a small number of laboratory accidents, doses of radiation given in radiotherapy, extrapolation from the results of animal experiments, and a study of about 250 people who were exposed to radiation from a test explosion in the Marshall Islands in 1954. There were, of course, no direct measurements made of radiation doses received at Hiroshima and Nagasaki, so they had to be estimated indirectly. The usually accepted estimates have now come under heavy criticism and are being revised. Meanwhile, the data have been reanalysed excluding those from Hiroshima and Nagasaki. The results suggest that the risk of cancer may be as much as five times higher than the figure quoted above.[16]

Of course, only people out in the open would be exposed to the full dose of radiation. Those in houses which were still standing would be protected to some extent from the radiation. Those in fallout shelters would be better protected to an extent which would depend on the materials from which the house or shelter was constructed. This is discussed in more detail later.

So far we have not considered the effect of a nuclear weapon destroying a nuclear power station. Not only would this increase the amount of radiation emitted immediately, but it would also have a much more serious effect in the long term as radioactivity arising from the destruction of a nuclear power station takes much longer to decay than that from a nuclear weapon. Some estimates of the effects are given in Bennett Ramberg's book *Destruction of nuclear energy facilities in war*.[17] As the book points out, power stations of all sorts are increasingly likely to become targets in both conventional and nuclear wars, and the greater accuracy of weapons means that attempts to hit them will become more likely to be successful. The book has, however, been criticised for not putting sufficient emphasis on the long term effects of attacks on nuclear power stations.[18]

This is an important omission, as radioactivity from reactors decays much more slowly than the radioactivity from nuclear weapons. If a nuclear reactor was attacked with a nuclear weapon, even a relatively small one, say 100 kilotons, the reactor would be vapourised and much of its radioactive content would be sucked up into the fireball and then deposited as fallout. Thus large areas would become uninhabitable for very long periods of time. Figure 3.6 gives estimates of the areas in which a person entering the area a month after the explosion and staying there for a year would receive doses of 10, 50 and 100 rads. The area within which a given dose is absorbed for a one megaton bomb exploding on a one GW(e) (1000 megawatt) reactor is very much greater than for a bomb alone. The areas affected by the explosion of the same size of bomb on a storage tank containing radioactive wastes are even larger.[19] The assumptions behind these estimates have, however, been criticised as being conservative, and it has been suggested that the areas could be even larger.[20]

Figure 3.6: **Areas affected by explosion of nuclear weapons alone and on nuclear power facilities**

Dose accumulated in one year starting one month after explosion	Area square miles		
	1 megaton bomb	1 megaton bomb on a storage tank	1 megaton bomb on a 1000 megawatt reactor
100	770	13100	23600
50	1550	17800	33600
10	9660	47100	63300

Source: Fetter and Tsipis, *Catastrophic nuclear radiation releases*[19]. Quoted in *Nuclear radiation in warfare*[13].

3.1.4 Electromagnetic pulse

Electromagnetic pulse (EMP) is an electromagnetic wave which results from secondary reactions when nuclear radiation is absorbed by molecules in the air or on the ground. It is a single very high voltage pulse which lasts for a very short time. There is no evidence that it can injure people directly, but it can wreck electrical and electronic systems. It is strongest when a bomb is exploded either at ground level or at a very high altitude, above 19 miles. If the explosion is at a very high altitude, electromagnetic pulse can cause damage over a radius of thousands of miles, as is shown in Figure 3.7. An explosion at an altitude of 62 miles would be more than sufficient to affect all of Great Britain and Ireland simultaneously.

The importance of EMP is its ability to cause severe damage in electrical components. For example, it can burn out transistors, destroy short wave radio and computer systems and cause disruptive instabilities in electrical systems such as power grids. The British telephone system is likely to be vulnerable to its effects. Because of this, it is not unlikely that in the event of a nuclear war, a weapon would be exploded at a very high altitude to disrupt an enemy's communications system. More details about EMP and its effects can be found in an article by Anthony Tucker[22] and in three articles in the American magazine *Science*.[21]

Figure 3.7: Distance from ground zero over which damage may be caused by electromagnetic pulse

Altitude of burst miles	Radius of area in which effects can occur miles	Area in which effects can occur sq miles
62	695	1 517 500
93	850	2 269 800
124	980	3 017 200
186	1195	4 486 300
249	1370	5 896 500
311	1520	7 258 300

Source: *The effects of nuclear weapons*[10]

3.2   HOW FAR WOULD THE POPULATION BE AFFECTED?

3.2.1.   What can we learn from the experience of Hiroshima and Nagasaki?

Estimates of the possible effects of a nuclear attack are bound to rely on data from Hiroshima and Nagasaki. Not surprisingly, there are a number of problems with this. The nature of the devastation caused by the bombs made it very difficult to assess how many people were killed outright, particularly in the areas near the centre of the explosions.

Some estimates rely on censuses taken in Japan in February 1944 and November 1945. People were, however, moving away from Hiroshima and Nagasaki between February 1944 and August 1945. It is also difficult to assess the extent to which the decrease in population as a result of the bomb deaths was inflated by survivors moving away from the devastated cities.

These problems are dicussed in detail in *Hiroshima and Nagasaki*[1]. The book gives a table showing a variety of estimates of the numbers of dead and missing persons. These range from 42 550 to 165 900 at Hiroshima and from 21 672 to 73 884 at Nagasaki. It is pointed out that the various estimates were arrived at by different methods and using different assumptions about the populations at risk. Some relate only to civilians while others include military personnel. Finally, some are confined to deaths immediately after the attacks, while others include those who died later.

Hiroshima and Nagasaki gives another table estimating that 118 661 civilians had died at Hiroshima by August 10 1946 while 3677 were missing, 30524 severely injured and 48 606 slightly injured out of a population of 320 081. In contrast to this, estimates given in the American book *The effects of nuclear weapons*[10] are that 68 000 civilians died and 76 000 were injured out of a total population of 256 300. While the book describes these lower estimates as "the best available", it does not specify the time period to which they apply.

In the first weeks and months after the attacks, the large numbers of patients and the lack of facilities made accurate record keeping impossible, so data about this period should be treated with some caution. In 1946 the United States sponsored Atomic Bomb Casualty Commission was set up to study the after effects on the populations of Hiroshima and Nagasaki, which it did in cooperation with the Japanese National

Institute of Health. A number of studies were done, mainly on small samples.

It was not until 1950 that a full survey of atomic bomb survivors was done, as part of the 1950 census. A sample of survivors was selected and this sample is still being followed up by the Radiation Effects Research Foundation which was set up in 1975 and is jointly sponsored by the Japanese and American governments. Data from this and other studies done by the Foundation are of a much higher quality than those collected earlier. They do, however have to rely on estimating people's radiation doses using information collected in 1950, five years after the exposure took place.

Even if more accurate data were available for Hiroshima and Nagasaki, the extent to which they could be extrapolated to other times and places would still be limited. The effects of the explosions were highly dependent on the weather, the terrain, the type of buildings and the circumstances on the days the bombs fell. For example, if the attacks had occurred in winter, fewer people would have been out of doors and they would have been wearing heavier clothing, so the effects might have been less severe.

More importantly, the weapons available today are much larger than the 12.5 kiloton bomb dropped on Hiroshima and the 22 kiloton bomb used at Nagasaki. In addition, only two cities were involved, thus help was available from outside for rescue work and reconstruction.

3.2.2. Scenarios for nuclear war

The effects of nuclear war makes estimates, assuming given sets of conditions, of the possible effects of nuclear attacks on Detroit and Leningrad both of which have populations of about 4 300 000. It was calculated that if a one megaton bomb exploded at ground level in Detroit, there could be 250 000 fatalities, 500 000 people injured and seventy square miles of property destroyed.

This scenario is somewhat unrealistic as it assumes that only these two cities are attacked. As we have suggested earlier, it is likely that a countercity attack would be much more extensive. The consequences of such an attack on this country would probably be worse than would be the case for the United States or the Soviet Union as our country is more densely populated and the potential targets are therefore much closer together. In the United States or the Soviet Union, there is at least a theoretical possibility of protecting some of the population by evacuating cities, or a little hope that some parts of the countries might escape the effects of the attack. These considerations are irrelevant in Britain as was brought home by a NATO exercise in 1980 which illustrated the sort of attack for which the Government is likely to be preparing.

3.2.3 Operation "Square Leg"

Operation "Square Leg" was carried out by NATO in September 1980. The scenario it envisaged was both a "counterforce" and a "countercity" attack as targets included both urban industrial centres and strategic targets such as airfields (particularly US bases), ports, depots, communications and command and control centres.[23]

It was assumed that a nuclear attack followed a period of tension during which, on September 12 1980, the Cabinet approved the suspension of parliament and assumed Emergency Powers. This was followed by panic buying by the public, and on September 15, war was declared. Many people would doubtless attempt to leave major population centres and areas close to military areas, despite government exhortation to stay where they were. The fourteen major roads out of London would be designated "Essential Service Routes" and reserved exclusively for government traffic. It is not clear what sanctions would be used against those attempting to use these routes but it seems unlikely that peaceful measures would be successful against large numbers of frightened people. It would be against a background of increasing panic therefore, that a nuclear attack was assumed to occur on September 19, the first strike falling between noon and 12.15 and the second between 1 and 3 pm. It was assumed that just under 100 weapons were dropped on 70 targets in England, and 7 targets in Wales were attacked. Twenty four bombs were assumed to have fallen on Scotland. No details have been released about attacks on Ireland.[24]

An article in the *New Scientist*[25] analysed the blast effects. The author did not have details of the weapon sizes which varied from 0.5 to 3 megatons, with a few 5 megaton explosions. He therefore assumed that all the bombs were of one megaton, which was likely to be an underestimate. Even this conservative estimate led to the conclusion that about 43 percent of the land area of England would be affected to some extent by blast but this area contained 60 percent of the population. Three of the seven bombs assumed to land on Wales did so in densely populated parts of South Wales. A separate article about the exercise in Scotland[24] showed that the attacks were concentrated on the Strathclyde and Lothian Regions which contain 47 percent and 14 percent of the population of Scotland respectively.[26] In this context, the Home Office's estimate in its pamphlet *Domestic Nuclear Shelters*[5] that 80 percent of the land area of the United Kingdom (which includes Northern Ireland) might not be affected by blast is irrelevant. It would seem that the areas affected by blast would be the more densely populated ones.

This was admitted by the Deputy Director of the Home Office Scientific Advisory Branch in a paper given at the British Association for Advancement of Science[2]. He assumed a multiple nuclear attack on Britain of 179 weapons with a total power of nearly 200 megatons – he did not say whether the scenario was the same as that in Operation "Square Leg". In his scenario the A and B rings, which are assumed to be exposed to peak overpressures of 6 psi and over, contain five percent of the land area but nearly 40 percent of the population.

3.2.4. The attack on London in Operation "Square Leg"

To illustrate what this would mean in detail, we present estimates of the effects on Greater London, whose boundaries contain 14 percent of the population of England.[27] Figure 3.8 gives the places, sizes and heights of the nuclear explosions for the bombs

Figure 3.8: Description of nuclear explosions in "Operation Square leg" with major effects on Greater London

Target	Power	Altitude of explosion	Time
	Megatons	ft	GMT
Heathrow	1	Surface	12.15
Heathrow	2	12000	12.15
Croydon	3	Surface	12.04
Brentford	2	Surface	12.06
Potters Bar	3	14000	13.30

Source: *The possible consequences of a nuclear attack on London*[33]

which were assumed in the "Square Leg" exercise to land within Greater London. Some of them would also affect areas outside the Greater London boundaries. Two other bombs assumed to land on Ongar and Sevenoaks would have led to some relatively light blast damage in North East and South East London respectively. What follows, however is an attempt to assess the effects on Greater London of the bomb attacks indicated in Figure 3.8.

The casualty estimates have been based on single warheads, an assumption which is likely to lead to conservative estimates of injuries and deaths. Single warheads would damage a smaller total area than multiple warheads of the same total explosive power.

The sizes of the overpressure contours were calculated using formulae given in *The effects of nuclear weapons*,[10] as was done to construct Figure 3.1. The rings corresponding to overpressure contours are shown superimposed on a map of London in Figure 3.9. The data shown in Figure 3.1 were then used to estimate the blast casualties in each overpressure ring.

The population within each overpressure ring was estimated using 1971 Census data for the population living in each 1 kilometre square of the National Grid.[28] Estimates of the numbers of fatalities and injuries among people living in Greater London are given in Figure 3.10. Because the areas likely to be affected by the blasts overlap, a range of estimates is given. The lower estimate assumes that the overpressures from more than one bomb are not additive, while the higher estimate assumes that they are, a much more likely assumption in practice. Indeed it may be that a simple additive model underestimates the combined effects of the two blasts.

Figure 3.11 gives two estimates of the numbers of people living in Greater London who would receive burn injuries. One estimate assumes that only one percent of the people who survived the initial effects of the blast were in the open and the other that 25 percent were in the open. In a situation such as that envisaged in "Square Leg", in which war had already been declared, it is quite possible that, despite exhortations to stay put, quite large numbers of people would attempt to get out of London and thus could be out of doors when the bombs fell. Use of census data does, however assume that they would be at home.

A theoretical pattern of the distribution of the fallout from the ground burst is shown in Figure 3.12. The ellipses indicate the areas within which accumulated doses of 1500 and 5000 rads would be emitted over two weeks, if, as Operation "Square Leg" assumed, the wind blew from the south. As was mentioned earlier, the patterns would not be so regular in practice.

It seems unlikely that any worthwhile monitoring of fallout levels could be done in these circumstances. The necessary equipment and people to operate it would have to be protected from the blast and heat, and the people would have to be protected from the fallout. Because of the unpredictability of the fallout pattern, either there would have to be a great many people monitoring it, or the people doing the task would have to be very mobile – a virtual impossibility in these circumstances.

Many people would be unable to take the protective measures advocated by Civil Defence. They would pose particular problems for the disabled and the elderly – about 15 percent of the population of Greater London is aged over 65[29] and 14 per cent of the population is both aged 60 or over and living alone.[30] In addition, only 3.5 percent of buildings within the Greater London boundaries have basements, and about a third of these are basement flats to which other households in the building may not have access.[31] People living in flats, in particular those on the upper floors of blocks of houses will be poorly protected against blast and fallout. This is serious in Greater London where 30.1 percent of dwellings are purpose built flats and 11.5 percent are conversions to flats.[31]

Figure 3.9 Estimated blast effects of nuclear attacks on London in Operation "Square Leg"

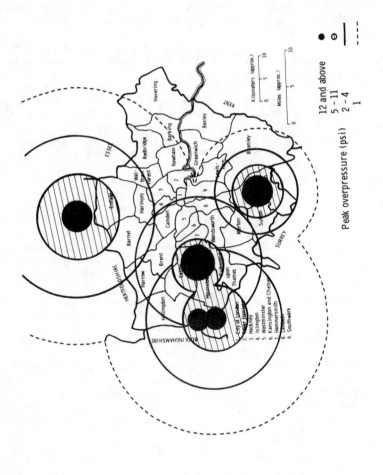

Figure 3.10: **Estimates of blast casualties to Greater London residents, resulting from bombs in Operation "Square Leg"**

	Persons affected millions
Immediate blast fatalities	1.1 +
Suffering from injuries due to blast	2.4 − 2.9
Uninjured by blast	3.1 − 3.6
Total GLC residents (1971)	7.1

Source: *The possible consequences of a nuclear attack on London.*[33]

Figure 3.11: **Estimates of numbers of Greater London residents who survive the blast and are injured by burns**

Overpressure ring psi	Types of burn	Persons with burns Assuming 1% outdoors	Assuming 25% outdoors
1	Some 2° many 1°	some	some
2 − 4	mainly 2° many 3°	28000	700 000
5 − 11	some 148 mainly 3°	5000	130 000

Source: *The possible consequences of a nuclear attack on London*[33]

Figure 3.12 Estimated fallout from nuclear attacks on London in Operation "Square Leg"

Accumulated dose 2 weeks after explosion

—— over 5000 rads   - - - 1500 - 5000 rads

All this means that the proportion of survivors of the initial effects of the bombs who could find effective shelter from the fallout is likely to be small. Many of those who do not would therefore die from the effects of fallout within the first few weeks after an attack. Individuals would not know how high a dose of radiation they had received. Since the early effects of radiation are not specific to it, it would be impossible to be sure at first whether a person was suffering from radiation sickness or vomiting because of stress or gastroenteritis. This would lead to widespread confusion amongst the medical workers attempting to look after the massive casualties.

The bombs envisaged in Operation "Square Leg" would destroy about 35000 of the 59000 hospital beds in Greater London. Of the 24000 which would remain, 10000 would be for psychogeriatric or mentally handicapped patients. Approximately 3500 general practitioners and 8000 hospital doctors work in London. Assuming that doctors died in the same proportion as the population as a whole, between 4000 and 6000 of these 11500 doctors would survive. Depending on the extent to which people who were injured in the blast also received burns, there would, on average, be between 400 and 900 patients per doctor, including anything from 6 to 175 major burns. If each doctor worked 18 hours a day and allowed 20 minutes per patient, it would take between 7 and 17 days to see them all.

The high levels of fallout would mean that many doctors who attempted to reach patients and patients who attempted to reach doctors would expose themselves to high levels of radiation in the process. Many doctors would not have relevant and recent training in dealing with the injuries involved. In addition, supplies of medicines and blood would soon run out, so the only treatment which could be offered would be simple surgery and the setting of broken bones, often without anaesthetics. Many people would die before any treatment at all reached them.

We can only conclude that medical care would be able to make very little impact on problems of this scale. It would appear that the planners of Operation "Square Leg" shared this view as they defined the technique of "triage". This means defining three categories of survivor: those who will survive without treatment, those who could survive with the simple treatment available and the rest. This third category, which would include people with radiation sickness, would receive no drugs or treatment.[32]

This scenario places particular emphasis on the implications for the medical profession, as it was originally prepared for a meeting of doctors.[33] Scientists Against Nuclear Arms is working on a version which also explores other effects, such as sanitation.

3.2.5 How to construct your own scenario

The data we have presented can be used to illustrate the effects of a one megaton bomb exploded either at ground level, or at an altitude of 8 000 feet. These are the main steps to take:

(i) Choose a likely target. The "Activities planning map" published by CND is a useful guide to military and other targets. Whether it is more reasonable to assume an air or a surface burst depends on the nature of the target. If it includes underground installations, it would be more reasonable to assume a ground level explosion.

(ii) Obtain population data for the areas round the target. The method used in the Greater London example was very laborious in that it involved adding up the populations of numerous one kilometre square areas. It was also expensive, as the data are unpublished and had to be bought from the Office of Population Censuses and Surveys (OPCS). Similar data from the 1981 Census will not be produced for some time and will be even more expensive. Given the inherent inaccuracy of the whole exercise, it would probably be sufficient to use the 1981 Census data on the population of each local authority district. These have been published in the preliminary reports for Scotland[26] and for England and Wales[27 34]. In addition, data about the age distribution of the population and the numbers of households containing only pensioners are being published for local areas from late 1981 onwards. In Scotland the reports are known as "Regional bulletins", and in England and Wales they are called "County monitors" (Series CEN 81 CM). There are plans to publish preliminary and county reports on the Northern Ireland Census at various times in 1982.

Some local authority areas are relatively large, so it will be necessary to use local knowledge about the way the population is distributed. Some county and district councils make estimates of the populations of the towns and villages within each local government district, and it may be possible to obtain these.

(iii) Find maps of suitable size. The Ordnance Survey's 1:50000 series maps show boundaries of local authority areas, but are on too large a scale for drawing the areas likely to be affected by a one megaton bomb.

(iv) The distances shown in Figure 3.1 can be used to draw circles to represent the blast contours and Figure 3.2 can be used to indicate the type of damage likely to occur at various distances from the centre of the explosion. Figure 3.1 can be used to estimate the casualties and injuries to people living within the areas exposed to each range of peak overpressures.

(v) Figure 3.3 can be used to indicate the thermal effects, and the data in Figure 3.1 can be used to derive ranges of estimates of numbers of burns amongst people who survived the blast effects.

(vi) If the explosion is assumed to be at ground level, Figure 3.4 can be used to draw theoretical fallout patterns. It is probably more realistic to assume that the prevailing wind is from the west south west, than to follow Operation "Square Leg" which assumed that it is from the south. Alternatively the fallout plume could be drawn on an overhead projector foil and rotated to illustrate the way changes in the wind direction can affect expected radiation doses.

(vii) Mark facilities such as water pumping stations, sewage treatment plants, hospitals etc. indicating the likely damage to them. Information about the type and location of hospitals and the numbers of beds they contain are published in the Medical Directory.[35] While some Regional Health Authorities publish statistics about the numbers of doctors and nurses who work in each hospital, it is rather more difficult to assess the way general practitioners and community nurses are distributed throughout the area, although Family Practitioner Committees publish lists of general practitioners and addresses of their surgeries.

3.2.6. Other scenarios

While Operation "Square Leg" assumed a full scale attack with relatively large weapons, the possibility of a theatre nuclear war, fought with smaller nuclear weapons has also been put forward. The United Nations Comprehensive Study of Nuclear Weapons[9] discusses several possible scenarios for this. In one it was assumed that 200 100 kiloton weapons and 1500 low yield weapons were used, with 50 per cent of the 100 kiloton and ten percent of the low yield weapons exploding at ground level. It was estimated that the number of civilians dead and severely injured by the immediate effects, the early fallout and the late radiation would be between six and seven million, while the total numbers of military personnel similarly affected would be 400000. Thus civilian casualties would be at least 12 times more numerous than military casualties.

There are other possible scenarios which do not seem to be mentioned. For example, if nuclear weapons were exploded under water at selected points round the coast, the entire country could be drenched in dense fallout.

3.3 LONG TERM EFFECTS

"The effects of nuclear war that cannot be calculated in advance are at least as important as those which analysts attempt to quantify."

This is one of the main conclusions of *The effects of nuclear war*[8], and it is likely to be an understatement. After the sort of attack on Britain envisaged in Operation "Square Leg", it would be likely that there would be a total breakdown of supplies of gas, electricity, coal and petroleum based fuels. Supplies of food and medicine would soon run out. Water supplies would be disrupted. They rely heavily on pumping systems and, in addition, river water has to be specially treated before it can be added to the water supply. In the Metropolitan Water Division which supplies much of Greater London, only 13 percent of the water comes from springs and boreholes, and the remaining 87 percent comes from rivers.[36] Sewage disposal and treatment would also break down.
    This is of critical importance, because the introduction of clean water and of sewerage systems played a major part in the decline of infectious disease in this country. Yet these diseases have not been totally eradicated,[37] and the aftermath of a nuclear attack would offer conditions in which they would be very likely to spread, while at the same time the facilities to treat them would not exist. People suffering from radiation sickness would be particularly susceptible to these infections. The overall prospect is that many people, especially those weakened by burns or other injuries, would die from thirst, starvation, exposure and infection.

Figure 3.13: Provision of food for survivors of nuclear war

Population (Survivors) (million) [current population: 54]	Arable land requirement[1] (million acres) [current arable land available: 18.3[2]]
50	20.9
45	18.8
40	16.7
30	12.5
20	8.4
10	4.2

1. Assumes each survivor needs 1670 plant calories per day (1470 calories from vegetables and 200 plant calories from ½ oz meat ration) and each arable area produces 4000 plant calories per day (½ the current level of production reflecting increased difficulty in farming after a war).
2. Clearly a nuclear attack would render some arable land unusable but would be expected to reduce the population more rapidly than the available land.

Source: *Beneath the City Streets*[39]

A study of the effects of a countercity strike on Britain[38] suggested that from half to two thirds of the people employed in papermaking, printing, shipbuilding, law, teaching, medicine, general engineering, vehicle manufacture, local government and building would be killed, as would two thirds to three quarters of those employed in precision instrument making, electrical engineering, insurance, banking, finance and national government. It is clear that a society lacking in these facilities would be very different from the one we know.

Peter Laurie in his book *Beneath the city streets*[39] does suggest, however, that, in the long term, some form of life might be possible. For example, Figure 3.13 claims that there could, in theory, be adequate food supplies, despite the fact that we import 55 percent of our food. The picture it paints does appear somewhat optimistic. For example, modern varieties of cereals have been bred with mechanical harvesting equipment in mind and are usually grown using fertilisers. Whether they would yield so well when more primitive methods are used is open to question. There would, however, be a much smaller population to feed than at present. All the same, the availability of supplies would be dependent on the existence of sufficient organisation to cultivate the remaining arable land and to distribute supplies. It is the existence, in the aftermath of a nuclear attack, of such a form of organised society which is the most problematic.

3.4   MITIGATING THE EFFECTS? CIVIL DEFENCE

3.4.1   Expenditure on Civil Defence

The money spent by the government on Civil Defence has varied considerably since the end of World War II. The peak era for expenditure came in the early 1950s and it was around this time that deep shelters for the protection of the government were constructed in London. Ironically, this era preceded the explosion of the H-bomb and after that time, spending on Civil Defence declined dramatically, possibly reflecting the establishment assumption of mutual assured destruction (MAD) in which Civil Defence would be largely irrelevant. In 1967, the Rescue and First Aid sections of the Civil Defence Corps were abolished and in 1968 the corps was abolished completely.

Recently, there has been a revival of interest in Civil Defence, accompanied by increased expenditure; though even the levels of £40 million per annum projected for the 1980s[40] shown in Figure 3.14 come nowhere near the levels (in current price terms) in

Figure 3.14:   **Expenditure on Civil Defence**

£ million at 1980 prices

	Financial Year								
Expenditure	75/6	76/7	77/8	78/9	79/80	80/81	81/2	82/3	83/4
capital	13	7	1	1	17	3	6		
current	16	16	14	14	15	17	23		
Total	30	23	15	15	32	20	29	40	40

Source: *The government's expenditure plans 1981/82 to 1983/84*[40]

the early 1950s. The increased spending may reflect increasing tension resulting from the "hotting-up" of the Cold war, or, more disturbingly, may reflect a shift in attitude away from MAD toward the concept of a "limited" (winnable) nuclear war.

As was the case for military expenditure, information on the objectives of this increased spending is barely available and the available information may be distorted. Some inkling is given by the fact that most of the expenditure is current, for example on emergency planning staff employed by local authorities, rather than capital cost. This indicates that little in the way of nuclear shelter construction is being undertaken. The only visible product of expenditure on civil defence takes the form of various pamphlets such as *Domestic nuclear shelters,*[5] the controversial *Protect and survive*[41] and the more recent *Civil defence, why we need it.*[42]

3.4.2. Government strategy for Civil Defence

The publication of pamphlets telling private individuals how to construct their own shelters, coupled with the lack of capital expenditure, shows that the government is pursuing a "self help" policy, rather than aiming towards provision of shelters for the whole population. Furthermore, *Civil defence, why we need it* calls for more volunteers to help paid emergency planning staff, commenting that reviving the old Civil Defence Corps "would cost an unjustifiable amount of money".[42]

Another indication of government strategy is given by the concentration on advice for shelter construction rather than evacuation planning. This is in contrast to the US civil defence program which envisages mass evacuation from cities, largely using private cars. Great Britain, unlike the US, is too small and densely populated for an evacuation strategy to succeed. The film *The war game* shows that, at one stage, evacuation was part of the government civil defence strategy, but this has now been abandoned.[12 32 42]

Given that other countries, notably Switzerland, attempt to make mass provision of fall-out shelters, the question arises as to why this country does not follow suit. Until recently, the doctrine of MAD would have provided justification for saving "wasted expense". If the government accepts the concept of a "limited" nuclear war, this justification disappears. In *Civil defence, why we need it,*[42] however, the Government claims that "The risk of war is at present considered so slight that the enormous cost of providing shelters to every family in the land could not be justified. It would cost billions of pounds".

We cannot establish the cost of a full shelter programme, but estimates range from £300 billion in *Beneath the city streets*[39] to £6.75 billion in *Protect and survive monthly.*[43] The Home Office's own estimates fall between these two extremes.[2] In any case, it is clear that the cost would be enormous. Even the Trident missile programme is expected to cost "only" £6 billion, although the estimates of costs continue to rise. To any government committed to reduction of public expenditure, a "self-help" policy is the only option. Even if we accept that there would be some point in spending vast sums of money on civil defence preparations, and the evidence we have seen for this is dubious, there is an additional danger for a nuclear power to embark on a civil defence "spending spree". If a country with nuclear strike capacity dramatically increases expenditure with a view to evading the consequences of nuclear retaliation, this might be interpreted by other countries as a form of aggression. Given the unstable world in which we live, such actions might increase international tensions to the point of precipitating attack. For countries such as Sweden and Switzerland, who do not possess nuclear weapons, provision of nuclear shelters is not so likely to be seen as aggressive.

In the event, the only shelters that have been constructed by the government are those designated for the Sub-regional Headquarters (SRHQs) and the Armed Forces

Headquarters (AFHQs) which since 1972 have taken over the functions of the more civilian oriented designated Regional Seats of Government (RSGs). These are the command centres for the system of government planned in the event of nuclear attack. The UK is divided into twelve regions: nine English regions, Wales, Scotland and Northern Ireland. English regions are sub-divided into two sub-regions each, Wales is divided into two zones and Scotland into three. The sub-regional governments will contain "representatives of almost all government departments, the police, fire service, elecricity, gas, water, hospital service, the BBC, the GPO and also local leading figures in industry who are given authority to organise their surviving colleagues in petrol, transport, building and food distribution".[39] It would appear that the main thrust of civil defence planning so far has been "control" rather than "survival" of the population. Within three days of the start of the "Scrum Half" exercise, the predecessor to "Square Leg", every army and police unit involved had notionally been supplied with CS gas munitions to help keep order.[44]

3.4.3 Going it alone: domestic nuclear shelters

Immediate effects As discussed earlier, the four main effects of a nuclear explosion which cause injury or death are blast, thermal radiation, initial radiation and, less instantly, fallout. Of the three immediate effects, a research study[25] has estimated that the largest lethal radii (the distance from ground zero within which certain fatality occurs) for unprotected persons are attributable to thermal effects for missiles over 20KT. Figure 3.15 shows the extent by which these lethal radii have been estimated to change for two types of fallout shelter: a basement shelter recommended for construction with 8-inch unreinforced concrete blocks and an underground shelter which would withstand 30 psi peak overpressure with shielding equivalent to 12 inches of concrete and 30 inches of earth. (Construction of this latter shelter would clearly be beyond the capabilities of the

Figure 3.15: Lethal radii in Miles from Ground Zero (Air Bursts and Surface Bursts)

Miles

Size of missile	Unprotected		Degree of Shelter Basement Shelter		Underground Shelter	
	Air	Surface	Air	Surface	Air	Surface
1 KT	0.51	0.53	0.32	0.31	0.06	0.11
20 KT	1.06	0.89	0.71	0.55	0.15	0.29
400 KT	3.67	2.27	2.98	1.88	0.41	0.80
1 MT	5.73	3.52	4.66	2.90	0.56	1.08
3 MT	9.25	5.72	7.64	4.72	0.81	1.56
5 MT	11.72	7.16	9.60	5.91	0.96	1.85
10 MT	16.05	9.77	13.35	8.18	1.21	2.33
20 MT	22.10	13.41	18.24	11.14	1.52	2.93

Source: *Estimates of the Kill Probability in target Area Family Shelters*[45]

average person – however motivated.) For the basement shelter, thermal effects still account for the largest lethal radii and distances are *not* reduced to any great extent. Interestingly, the table published by the Home Office in their pamphlet *Domestic Nuclear Shelters*[5] which compares the relative protection given by various types of nuclear shelters, does not mention the effects of thermal radiation!

Fallout Though a shelter which could be constructed by an average person would hardly give protection from the immediate effects of a nuclear explosion, such shelters can give protection against fallout. It has been estimated that anyone remaining unprotected within seventy miles downwind of ground zero for the first two weeks after the explosion of a one megaton bomb, would have less than 50 percent chance of surviving the fallout.[10] The chance of survival is greatly increased for persons under shelter of some kind; the degree of protection depending on the construction and design of the shelter.

Figure 3.16: Thickness of material required to give a protective factor of 2[1]

Material	Thickness inches
Lead	0.5
Steel	0.7
Tiles	1.0 – 1.9
Corrugated asbestos sheet	2.0
Asphalt	2.2
Concrete	2.2
Stone	2.2
Brickwork	2.8
Sand	2.9
Earth	3.3
Plaster	3.5
Slates	3.5
Wood	8.8

1. The protective factor increases geometrically with the thickness of the material
   eg 4.4 inches of concrete gives a protective factor of 4
   6.6 inches of concrete gives a protective factor of 8

Source: *Domestic nuclear shelters*[5]

The protection given by buildings or shelters can be expressed in terms of "protective factors" (PF); a PF of ten, for example, implies that anyone sheltering in a building of this PF would receive a radiation dose reduced to one-tenth of that received by an unprotected person. Figure 3.16 shows the relative thickness of various construction materials required to give a PF of two. Figure 3.17 shows the Home Office estimates of the PF of various types of housing and, for comparison, the PF of the four types of shelter discussed in the pamphlet *Domestic Nuclear Shelters*.[5] [7] It is worth noting that the estimated PF given by the type I (improvised) shelter is rather less than that given by a refuge room in many types of housing, particularly terraced houses. Knowledge of these statistics might save many people from a lot of futile digging! Figure 3.18 shows how the

Figure 3.17: Approximate protective factors in ground floor refuge rooms of typical British housing[1] and of domestic shelters described in Domestic Nuclear Shelters

Type of shelter	Protective factor
Bungalow	5 – 10
Detached two-storey	15
Semi-detached two-storey 11 inch cavity walls	25 – 30
Semi-detached two-storey 13½ inch brick walls	40
Type 1 (improvised) nuclear shelter	not less than 40
Terraced two-storey	45
Terraced back-to-back	60
Type 2 (indoor kit) nuclear shelter	not less than 70
Blocks of flats and offices: lower floors	50 – 500
second floor and above	50-20
Type 3 (outdoor kit) nuclear shelter	not less than 200
Type 4 (purpose built) nuclear shelter	over 300

1. Assuming timber upper floors and with windows and external doors blocked.

Source: *Domestic nuclear shelters*[5] and *Nuclear weapons*[6]

accumulated radiation dose at two weeks would change for persons sheltered by different values of PF from a one-megaton bomb. For PFs of 20 (within the protection given by many types of housing) the accumulated dose at two weeks of a person sheltered 23 miles downwind is reduced to 250 rads which is less than the LD50, although most people would still suffer from radiation sickness and a substantial proportion (10-20%) would die without medical attention. At 53 miles downwind of ground zero, people sheltered with a protection factor of 10 (given by most housing) would be unlikely to suffer even radiation sickness, although the long-term effects of radiation, such as genetic damage would still be a danger.

To say that it would not be impossible to protect ourselves from fallout is a long way from implying that such protection would be easily achieved or that the process involved would be anything but extremely unpleasant. We do not know the assumptions on which the Home Office estimates of the PFs of refuges/shelters are based but they are likely to assume that shelters are perfectly constructed, ie that all windows are blocked up and sand-bags in place, etc. It is also assumed that no-one ever leaves the shelter during the fallout period, as PFs are sharply reduced if you venture outside even for a short time. As it is not likely that a "do-it-yourself" shelter would be anything like spacious or, in the circumstances, have adequate sanitary arrangements, continuous existence in the

Figure 3.18: Fallout from a 1 Megaton surface explosion[1]: radiation dose exposure at two weeks for different protective factors

rads

Downwind	Un-Protected	Protective factor							
		10	20	30	40	50	60	100	200
23	5000	500	250	167	125	100	83	50	25
53	1000	100	50	33	25	20	17	10	5
71	600	60	30	20	15	12	10	6	3
127	200	20	10	7	5	4	3	2	1
179	100	10	5	3	2.5	2	2	1	0.5

1. Assuming 50 per cent of energy of explosion derived from fission

Source: *The effects of nuclear weapons*[10]

shelter for a fortnight would be extremely unappetising, even ignoring such factors as the possibility of sickness from radiation poisoning. For a more detailed description of the realities of life in a domestic shelter, see the CND pamphlet *Civil Defence: the cruellest confidence trick*.[46] Figure 3.19 presents a list of the food and other necessities recommended by the Home Office for fourteen days survival.[5] Even if it were possible to obtain all the stores listed, they would require a large amount of space, making the environment even more cramped. The list should be read in the context that the space allotted per person in a type 1(a) shelter described in the same pamphlet is 3' × 2½' × 3½'.[15] Apart from questions of discomfort, there are many other reasons why people would be forced to leave their shelters and accumulate radiation. The government assumes that medical staff would be available to treat the injured; to do so they would have to spend considerable periods unprotected – which would not enhance their chances of long-term survival. Volunteers would be required to put out fires etc. and people generally would wish to go to the assistance of friends and relatives. The true protection attained through domestic nuclear shelters is therefore likely to be very much lower than the government estimates.

3.4.4. Long-Term Civil Defence
Those people who survived the immediate effects of a nuclear attack and the later fallout, would emerge into a world totally different from the one they knew – and one in which life-expectancy would be considerably reduced! In the medium term, as we mentioned earlier, sanitary facilities, energy supplies and food would not be generally available and many people would probably die later from disease compounded by weakness due to radiation poisoning or starvation. It would be in this period that the regional governments would emerge above ground and start "organising" the survivors – though with a system of controls likely to rely heavily on the use of force. There seems to be no mention of civil defence planning to minimise the spread of disease, but the government apparently keeps strategic food stocks in fifty or so "buffer depots" which could be used to stave off mass starvation for a time, assuming that distribution problems could be overcome.

Figure 3.19: Provisions and other necessities for 14 days in a nuclear shelter

Quantities per person

Water	56 pints
Biscuits, crackers, breakfast cereals etc	6 lb (2750g)
Canned meat or fish	4¼lb (2000g)
Canned vegetables	4lb (1800g)
Canned margarine or butter, peanut butter	1lb (500g)
Jam, marmalade, honey or spread	1lb (500g)
Canned soups	6 cans
Full cream evaporated milk or dried milk	14 small cans or 2x½lb containers
Sugar	1½lb (700g)
Tea or coffee (instant)	½lb (250g)
Sweets	1lb (450g)
Radio	
Tin opener, bottle opener, cutlery, crockery and cooking utensils	
Warm clothing	
Bedding	
Torch	
Toilet articles, First aid kit, washbowls, cleaning materials	
Note-book for noting radio instructions (! sic)	
Spade	
Toilet equipment	
Clock and calendar	

Source: *Domestic nuclear shelters* [5]

Little can be postulated about the long-term prospects for survivors because they would depend so heavily on the degree of nuclear attack and the extent to which nuclear war had spread world-wide. In all events, it seems transparently clear that our long term future, and indeed our chances of having any future at all, would be better safeguarded by efforts to prevent the outbreak of nuclear war than by any planning to mitigate the effects after a nuclear attack.

References

1. The Committee for the compilation of materials on damage caused by the atomic bombs in Hiroshima and Nagasaki. *Hiroshima and Nagasaki. The physical, medical and social effects of the atomic bombings.* Tokyo : Iwanami Shoten. 1979. English edition translated by Eisei Ishikawa and David Swain. Hutchinson. 1981.
2. Butler SFJ. *Scientific advice in home defence.* Paper given to the British Association for the Advancement of Science. 1981.
3. Hitchens C. A do-it-yourself guide to death. In: *Britain and the bomb. NS Report 3.* London: New Statesman. 1981.
4. *The Leveller. No. 60.* July 10-24 1981.
5. Home Office. *Domestic nuclear shelters. Technical guidance.* London: HMSO. 1981.
6. Home Office and Scottish Home and Health Department. *Nuclear weapons.* London: HMSO. 1974.
7. Goodwin P. *Nuclear war the facts on our survival.* London: Ash and Grant. 1981.
8. Office of Technology Assessment. Congress of the United States. *The effects of nuclear war.* Allunheld, New Jersey: Osmun Montclair and London: Croom Helm. 1980.
9. *Comprehensive study on nuclear weapons.* New York: United Nations. 1981.
10. Glasstone S, Dolan PJ. *The effects of nuclear weapons.* Washington: United States Department of Defence and United States Department of Energy. 1977.
11. Lifton R. *Death in life.* New York: Random House. 1967.
12. McFarlane C. Neutron bomb, no respector of property. *Science for People 49.* Summer 1981. 10-13.
13. Rotblat J. *Nuclear radiation in warfare.* London: Taylor and Francis. 1981.
14. Langham WH. ed. *Radiobiological factors in manned space flight.* Washington DC: National Academy of Sciences. 1967.
15. United Nations Committee on the Effects of Atomic Radiation. *Sources and effects of ionizing radiation.* New York: United Nations. 1977.
16. Charles MW., Lindop PJ. Risk assessment without the bombs. *Journal of the Society for Radiological Protection 1981*; 1: 15-19.
17. Ramberg B. *Destruction of nuclear energy facilities in war.* Lexington Massachusetts: DC Heath. 1980.
18. Tucker A. Falling out over bombs. *Guardian.* April 4 1981. 11.
19. Fetter S, Tsipis K. Catastrophic nuclear radiation releases. *MIT Report No. 5.* Cambridge Massachusetts: MIT. 1980. Also summarised in *Scientific American 1981*; 244: 33-39.
20. Lindop P. Medical implications of nuclear disasters. *Proceedings of the Medical Association for Prevention of War 1981*; 3: 166-176.
21. Nuclear pulse. *Science* 1981; 212: 1009-1012, 1116-1120, 1248-1251.
22. Tucker A. Electromagnetic effects: the EMP and slow ionisation problem. In: Royal United Services Institute. *Civil Defence.* Pergamon. In the press.
23. Campbell D. World War III: an exclusive preview. In: *Britain and the bomb. NS Report 3.* London: New Statesman. 1981.
24. Campbell D. Scotland's nuclear targets. In: *Britain and the bomb. NS Report 3.* London: New Statesman. 1981.

25. Steadman P. The bomb: worse than the government admits. *New Scientist*. June 18 1981. 769-771.
26. Registrar General Scotland. *Census 1981, Scotland. Preliminary report*. Edinburgh: HMSO. 1981.
27. Office of Population Census and Surveys. *Census 1981. Preliminary Report. England and Wales*. CEN 81 PR (1). London: HMSO 1981.
28. Office of Population Census and Surveys. Unpublished data from the 1971 census.
29. Greater London Council. *1981 population projections*. London: GLC. 1981.
30. Department of the Environment. *National Dwelling and Housing Survey, 1978*. London: HMSO 1979.
31. Greater London Council. *Greater London Housing Conditions Survey. Reviews and studies series No. 7*. London: Greater London Council. 1981.
32. Campbell D. In place of civil defence. In: *Britain and the bomb. NS Report 3*. London: New Statesman. 1981.
33. Haines AP. *The possible consequences of a nuclear attack on London*. Paper presented at the First Congress of International Physicians for the Prevention of Nuclear War. Washington DC. March 1981.
34. Office of Population Censuses and Surveys. *Census 1981. Preliminary report for towns*. CEN 81 PR(2). London: HMSO. 1981.
35. *The Medical Directory*. London and Edinburgh: Churchill Livingstone. Published annually.
36. Metropolitan Water Division. *A description of the undertaking*. London: Thames Water Authority. 1980.
37. Office of Population Censuses and Surveys, Communicable Disease Surveillance Centre. *Communicable disease statistics 1979*. London: HMSO. 1981.
38. De Kadt E. *British defence policy and nuclear war*. 1964.
39. Laurie P. *Beneath the city streets*. London: Panther. 1979.
40. *The government's expenditure plans 1981/82 to 1983/84*. Cmnd 8175. London: HMSO. 1981.
41. *Protect and survive*. London: HMSO. 1980.
42. Home Office and Scottish Home and Health Department. *Civil defence, why we need it*. London: HMSO. 1981.
43. Sibley B. *Protect and survive monthly* 1981; 10: 18-20.
44. Campbell D. The dress rehearsal. In: *Britain and the bomb. NS Report 3*. London: New Statesman. 1981.
45. Russell P.W., Kimbrel L.G. Estimates of the kill probability in target area family shelters. *Journal of the American Medical Association 1962*; 180: 25-29. (April 7).
46. Bolsover P. *Civil defence: the cruellest confidence trick*. London: CND. 1981.

4 MOVING ON

4.1 INTRODUCTION

Most of the statistical arguments which occur in the nuclear weapons debate concern the interpretation of the situation now, in our nuclear world. In chapters one, two, and three we have been mainly concerned to discover ways in which official statistics pertaining to the state of the nuclear world and the effects of nuclear war are misleading. The final section of this chapter summarises the general problems of interpreting military statistics and the conclusions we draw from their examination.

Before doing this, however, we will comment briefly on the alternatives to nuclear strategies. The reason we devote such a short space to this very important issue is that statistics do not at present play a large part in it. As alternative defence strategies have generally yet to be tried, it is inevitable that there are fewer statistics which could clarify the issues.

4.2 DISARMAMENT

4.2.1. Conversion of industry from military to civil production

One of the influential arguments against cuts in defence spending (apart from the ever present "Russian threat") is the fear that jobs will be lost. In this country some 220 000 people work directly in the defence industries and about the same number are in employment which is indirectly dependent on military expenditure.[1] Without any alternative arrangement these people would lose their jobs in the event of disarmament, and it is the feasability of such alternatives that we consider in the following paragraphs. Alongside such conversion of military industries, disarmament could, with appropriate social policies, be translated into increased leisure and opportunities for retraining, without ever increasing unemployment.

There have been several American studies of the possibilities for conversion of industry away from military production. One undertaken for the US government[2] identified 55 industries suitable for conversion to civil production in the event of a one third cut in military spending. Dan Smith[3] quotes a study which estimates that only 13% of staff working on US military R and D would, in the event of general and complete disarmament, be able to move from their occupation to its direct civilian equivalent, eg from military to civil aerospace. It would, however, require an average of less than a year's retraining before almost all the rest could be employed in school teaching, government research, environmental protection, etc.

In this country various concrete suggestions have been put forward for the conversion of specific arms dependent industries. The best known is the *Lucas (Aerospace) Alternative Corporate Plan* published in 1976.[4] This suggested 150 alternatives to the military products which are made by the company. The suggestions included the development of alternative energy, medical, and transport technologies, all of which would build on the existing skills of Lucas workers. Other suggestions have been put forward for the Vickers combine. Reports have been published showing the possibilities for conversion in the shipbuilding section,[5] and for the Chieftain tank[6]. The report on the shipbuilding section recommends the development of new sea based technologies such as wave power and equipment for mining and agriculture on the sea bed. The report concluded "There is no reason to suppose that the export potential of these projects would be less than that of armaments". The Vickers studies make it clear, however, that conversion away from military production is subject to opposition from vested interests, and could not be achieved without substantial government intervention.

The potential for conversion means that there is no reason why cuts in military spending have to lead to unemployment. We are dubious, however, of the claims sometimes made that the number of people employed per unit of government expenditure is less for military than for other spending. In Figure 4.1. we show a US congressman's estimate of the number of people employed in different sectors for each billion dollars of government expenditure. It seems doubtful to us that this calculation has fully taken into account the people indirectly employed as a result of military spending. The high capital intensity of most military production means that much expenditure goes on manufacturing equipment rather than on direct labour costs. Those engaged in making this equipment *should* be included in an estimation of jobs dependent on government military expenditure.

Figure 4.1:   A US Congressman's estimates of number of people employed for
$1billion state expenditure

000s

Sector	Employees
"Public Service"	132
Education	100
Housing and Health	76
Defence	35

Source: Cited by Albrecht et al *A Short Research Guide on Arms and Armed Forces*
Croom Helm London 1978 p95

4.2.2.   Disarmament so far: multilateral treaties

Although as yet no steps have been taken towards general disarmament, treaties exist which have been designed to limit the use of some weapons, particularly nuclear weapons. Figure 4.2 lists the various arms limitation treaties in force on 31st December 1980. The six major multilateral nuclear arms control treaties and conventions were concluded with the following objectives:

(i) to prohibit the siting of nuclear weapons in certain areas (Antarctica, Latin America, outer space and the sea bed).

(ii) to restrict nuclear weapon tests.

(iii) to prevent the spread of nuclear weapons.

Figure 4.2: Major post-World War II arms limitation agreements in force on 31 December 1980

Treaty	Date signed	Brief description	No of parties as of 31/12/80
Antartic Treaty	1/12/59	Declares Antartica will be used exclusively for peaceful purposes.	21
Partial Test Ban Treaty	5/ 8/63	Bans nuclear tests in the atmosphere, outer space and under water (but not underground)	118
Outer Space Treaty	27/ 1/67	Prohibits placing of nuclear weapons in orbit, celestial bodies shall be used exclusively for peaceful purposes	82
Treaty of Tlatelolco	14/ 2/67	Establishes Latin America as a nuclear-free zone	22
Non-Proliferation Treaty	1/ 7/68	Prohibits acquisition of nuclear weapons by non-nuclear weapon states	114[1]
Sea-bed Treaty	11/ 2/71	Prohibits emplacement of nuclear weapons on the seabed beyond a 12 mile zone	70
Biological Weapons Convention	10/ 4/72	Prohibits biological warfare	91
SALT I ABM Treaty	26/ 5/72	Limits certain US and Soviet anti-ballistic missiles and ballistic missile launchers	
SALT I Interim Agreement	26/ 5/72		
Document on Confidence Building Measures	1/ 8/75	Provides for notification of major military manoeuvres in Europe.	
Environmental Modification Convention	18/ 5/77	Prohibits hostile use of techniques which could produce substantial environmental modifications	31

1. Egypt ratified in 1981, bringing the number up to 115.

Source: *SIPRI Yearbook of World Armaments and Disarmament 1981*

81

All of these treaties have their deficiencies and none of them provide for a *reduction* in the number of nuclear weapons. Furthermore they suffer from the disadvantage that not all countries are party to them. The Non-proliferation Treaty has the largest number of signatories but even so there are about a dozen countries who possess significant nuclear technology and have not signed the treaty. One of these, India, has conducted a nuclear explosion, as can be seen in Figure 4.3. Also, France and China, which did not sign the Partial Test Ban Treaty, have still been conducting atmospheric tests.

Figure 4.3: Nuclear explosions 1945-1980 (known and presumed)

Country	Number of explosions 16/7/45-5/8/63[1]	Number of explosions 5/8/63-31/12/80[2]	
		atmospheric	underground
USA	293	0	374[3]
USSR	164	0	283
UK	23	0	10
France	8	41	48
China	na	22	4
India	0	0	1

1. Date of signing of the Partial Test Ban Treaty prohibiting nuclear weapons tests in the atmosphere.
2. Data for 1980 are provisional.
3. Five devices used in the same test are counted here as one.

Source: *SIPRI Yearbook of World Armaments and Disarmament 1981*

While multilateral treaties have not been generally successful in halting the further development and deployment of nuclear weapons, or in reducing the nuclear arsenals held by the superpowers, they may serve as a focus for countries' and movements' non nuclear aspirations. Brazil and Argentina are, for example, likely to develop nuclear weapons despite the Treaty for the Prohibition of Nuclear Weapons in Latin America. Nevertheless those opposed to nuclear weapons in these and other countries in Latin America may be able to use the existence of the treaty to expose the hypocrisy of the governments concerned and to point the way forward to a genuine nuclear free zone.

4.2.3. Alternative Defence Strategies

As yet, no nation has renounced nuclear weapons after developing an independent nuclear arsenal. Non-nuclear defence strategies are not, however, uncommon among countries *capable* of producing nuclear weapons. Figure 2.1 shows that in Europe this is true of West Germany, Italy, Sweden and Switzerland. West Germany and Italy do allow US nuclear weapons to be stationed on their territory as NATO members. Canada, having previously deployed nuclear weapons as part of NATO nuclear strategy, has now ceased to do so – the first nation to take such a stand. The Canadian example demonstrates that a nation may decide to reject nuclear weapons while remaining in NATO. Norway and Denmark also forbid the deployment of nuclear weapons on their land in peacetime.

A policy of remaining in NATO but renouncing nuclear weapons may be thought contradictory for Britain because of its special role in the alliance. If Britain decided to base its defence policy outside the superpower blocks, it would not be the first European country to do so. Austria, Finland, Ireland, Sweden, Switzerland, and Yugoslavia all have such policies, although in the case of Austria and Finland the policy is enforced by treaty. The defence strategies of most of these countries rely on "Territorial" defence, the basis of which is to deter an attack by military plans designed to extract a heavy toll on an invading or occupying army. Militia or "home defence" forces play varying roles in the implementation of this strategy. Such defence plans cannot be seen as aggressive by other nations. We can compare the percentage of GDP spent on defence by Austria (1.2%), Sweden (3.3%), Switzerland (2.3%) and Yugoslavia (5.6%) with those given for NATO countries in Figure 2.7 (4.2% overall). Though not cheap, territorial defence is on average no more expensive than nuclear-based "defence". Switzerland also has a policy of providing shelters against fallout to guard against the effects of nuclear attacks on neighbouring countries. The shelters are not designed to provide protection against blast since Switzerland does not expect to be a nuclear target itself.

4.3   WHAT CAN WE LEARN FROM MILITARY STATISTICS?

It is hardly surprising that the data produced and published by governments should serve their purpose better than that of their critics. We have been concerned with the part played by statistics in defending policies to maintain and extend the role of nuclear weapons, and are able to expose some myths created by the misleading use of military statistics. We are less able to develop our own complete version of what is going on.

In the first part of this section we review some of the general problems encountered in interpreting military statistics. In the final part we summarise the doubts we have raised about many statistical claims made in support of nuclear weapons.

4.3.1.   What do statistics measure?

We have stressed both the dubious quality of much data concerned with nuclear war, and the misuse of them by those who advocate rearmament. Many of the problems with the data themselves are common to a wide range of statistics: problems of classification (what counts as "military"); of relevance (are Soviet troops stationed on the USSR-China border relevant to a NATO-WP comparison?); of international comparison (what exchange rate to use). What makes these problems particularly serious in the case of military data is the secrecy which is exercised by governments. This permits them to make public only the data which best serve their purposes. Chapter one in particular provides many examples, among them the great variation in estimates of Soviet arms expenditure, and the different estimates of strengths of "Eurostrategic" nuclear weapons given by the UK government and other sources.

The problem of whether statistics measure what they claim to measure is made worse by the question of whether what is measured is actually what we are interested in. For example in arguing for the existence of a "Soviet Threat", statistics are often given solely on military expenditure, levels of arms, etc, when "threat" is a concept involving many other factors. Figure 4.4 shows diagrammatically what the main such factors are. *Threat* depends partly, to be sure, on relative *capabilities*, but also on an assessment of an adversary's objectives, and the political constraints under which they must act. Similarly

Figure 4.4 What can you measure?

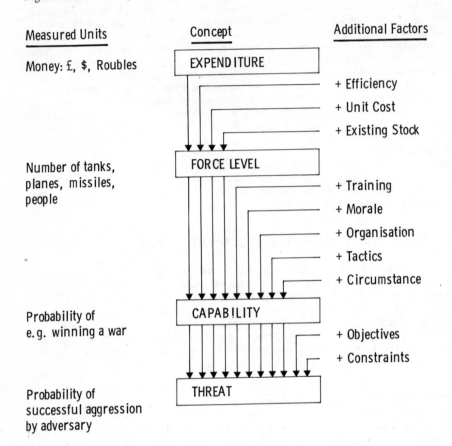

Measured Units	Concept	Additional Factors
Money: £, $, Roubles	EXPENDITURE	+ Efficiency + Unit Cost + Existing Stock
Number of tanks, planes, missiles, people	FORCE LEVEL	+ Training + Morale + Organisation + Tactics + Circumstance
Probability of e.g. winning a war	CAPABILITY	+ Objectives + Constraints
Probability of successful aggression by adversary	THREAT	

Source : Adapted from D. Smith and R. Smith
The Economics of Militarism
London   Pluto Press   Forthcoming (1982)

capability depends only partially on *force levels*, which only partially reflect *expenditure*. In practice only some of the relevant factors are measured by statistics, and the others are neglected or only wheeled out when convenient. *Expenditures* are regularly used as measures of *force levels*. These in their turn are used as measures of *capabilities*, which are then used to measure the *threat* faced. The more adventurous propagandist will happily leap over most of the items in the diagram to treat increased Soviet arms spending as a threat in itself.

In summary, when evaluating military data and the arguments they are used to support, it is important to have some idea how the data are produced so as to be able to see what is likely to be technically wrong with them. At the same time it is equally important to check that the data really measure the relevant concept and not some partial substitute.

4.3.2 The mythical arguments for nuclear weapons

Many of the conclusions of this pamphlet take the form of exposing as myths the claims made in support of nuclear weapons. While many would oppose nuclear arms irrespective of what the statistics say, the arguments *for* these weapons depend on showing the existence of a Soviet threat, the viability of deterrence, and so on. All these rest on statistics. In order to raise doubts among those who support Britain's continued possession of nuclear arms, the weakness of the statistical evidence for these claims should be spelt out.

NATO, its member governments, and their supporters in the media and elsewhere frequently argue that:

(i) *"Western military expenditure is less than the Soviet bloc's".*
Yet we have shown in Chapter 1 that governments can pick and choose among different estimates of expenditure, that estimates of Soviet expenditure are particularly dubious, that non-government sources suggest rough parity between NATO and the Warsaw Pact, and that in any case we cannot confuse the *cost* of "defence" with the *capability* that the money buys, as the rearmers often do.

(ii) *"The Soviet Union has a crucial superiority in tanks in Europe".*
But this neglects differences between the tanks, the emphasis by NATO on anti-tank weapons, the balance of other "theatre" weapons, and different practices with respect to scrapping obsolete tanks.

(iii) *"The Warsaw Pact has a crucial superiority in 'Eurostrategic' weapons."*
But this superiority is only in longer range weapons; if effectiveness rather than numbers of systems is compared, and NATO submarines in Europe are included, the disparity is greatly reduced; and in any case the relevance of such a conclusion for rearmament depends on a dubious division between a European "theatre" and a strategic superpower war.

(iv) *"Civilian use of nuclear power is a separate issue from that of nuclear weapons."*
But Chapter 2 shows that the export of civilian nuclear technology acts as a channel for the proliferation of nuclear weapons. This is happening much faster than any attempts to restrict them, thus multiplying the risk of nuclear war. Furthermore power stations would be a target in war, and the effect of attacking nuclear ones would be devastating.

(v) *"Military expenditure benefits us all."*
Profits from military production are limited to arms manufacturers and merchants. Furthermore arms production means lost opportunities for socially useful production and increased leisure particularly in those countries which can least afford it.

(vi) *"Britain could survive a nuclear war since the effects have been exaggerated."*
But while, as Chapter 3 shows, the precise effects of a nuclear war depend on particular

circumstances which are not predictable, the large number of military targets in Britain and the ineffectiveness of the civil defence programme mean that Britain would be completely devastated. Furthermore no conceivable civil defence programme could be effective as long as the targets remained in place.

(vii) *"A non-nuclear defence strategy is impossible."*
But there are increasing numbers of countries which have deliberately adopted such strategies, perhaps aware that a country that does not itself pose a nuclear threat would be much less likely to be attacked with nuclear weapons.

(viii) *"Disarmament even if desirable would make unemployment worse."*
But there have been several studies showing the viability of conversion from military to socially useful production. Besides which, labour released from arms production, if redistributed, could allow increased leisure for all.

Thus we conclude, in spite of all the claims to the contrary, that there is no sound statistical basis to the arguments for the retention of nuclear weapons, even less the acquisition of new ones.

References
1. *UK Government Statement on Defence 1981* London HMSO 1981 Vol 2 tables 1.2 and 5.2.
2. US Arms Control and Disarmament Agency. *Final Report on Industrial Conversion Potential in the Shipbuilding Industry.* March 1966.
3. D. Smith. *Principles of a Conversion programme.*
4. *Lucas– an Alternative Plan.* IWC pamphlet no. 55, Russell Press, Nottingham 1976.
5. *Alternative Employment for Naval Shipbuilding Workers.* Vickers Barrow Shop Stewards. Date not given.
6. *Building a Chieftain Tank and the Alternative.* Vickers National Combine Committee of Shop Stewards. Date not given.

APPENDIX: SOURCES OF STATISTICS

The purpose of this appendix is to summarise the available sources of statistics about the various military establishments, and to indicate their main shortcomings. Additional comments relating to specific numbers are contained in the rest of the pamphlet; what follows is intended to avoid repetition in the main text, as well as advise readers who want to explore the available statistics further. Military statistics, properly interpreted, can often help answer certain questions, but this depends on a critical examination of the context in which they are produced, and the omissions and misrepresentations which are likely to result.

Where do the data come from?

There are three main primary sources of military statistics:

(i) National governments' budget and services data, produced in the course of the administrative process, and to a greater or lesser extent published or made available in processed form.

(ii) Intelligence community estimates, based on electronic coverage, satellite surveillance, spying, guesswork, . . .

(iii) Academic research calculations, typically based on estimates derived from subjecting other data to critical scrutiny, although sometimes original research is involved.

There are very strong incentives to select or even distort the numbers from all three of these sources for propaganda purposes, since the numbers have signalling functions. But even for one organisation the incentives often work in opposite directions, so that the signalling becomes hopelessly confused. Thus, for example, the British government is eager to show NATO and the US that it is doing its bit by coming up with high estimates of its military expenditure – and equally keen to show the British public that it is keeping the cost of the military to a minimum, and/or that military spending is too low and should be increased. As a result a range of estimates is used selectively for different purposes.

More generally, there is particular scope for varying what is included as a "military" rather than a civilian activity. Airports, telecommunications systems, even hospitals may be employed for purposes which one would not guess at from their classification in official statistics. Furthermore methods of calculation tend to vary from year to year. The complications have become such that the Soviet government has now apparently given up, publishing the same figure for its military spending every year! All these factors are cited here to underline the need for great caution in relying on *any* military statistic. If this is borne in mind, quite a lot of useful information can be extracted from the mountains of self-justificatory pamphlets produced by the Ministry of Defence and by NATO. *The Annual Statement on the Defence estimates* is a particularly valuable British source.

Where are the data published?

The principal published sources of military statistics are the following:
(i) The Stockholm International Peace Research Institute (SIPRI), which publishes in particular the annual *SIPRI Yearbook of World Armaments and Disarmament*. This is a rather expensive volume but a good buy for libraries. It contains a survey of critical issues and developments as well as an extensive set of statistics. SIPRI also publishes a wide range of more specialised books and pamphlets; while very useful, they are often rather ploddingly presented and sometimes overly technical. (SIPRI, Sveavägen 166, S-11346 Sweden).
(ii) The US Arms Control and Disarmament Agency (ACDA), which relies mainly on data from the CIA. ACDA's publications, such as *World Military Expenditures and Arms Transfers*, contain brief and succinct summaries, well illustrated with graphs and charts, in addition to their statistical tables. There is no attempt to hide the origins of data on Soviet activities, i.e. from the CIA, and indeed there is even some discussion of alternative estimation procedures. (ACDA, Washington, D.C. 20451, USA).
(iii) The London-based International Institute of Strategic Studies (IISS) uses data from diplomatic, military and intelligence sources, and its annual *Military Balance* and *Strategic Survey* have recently been criticised in CND and related quarters as reflecting too unquestioningly the NATO point of view.

None of the figures from any of these three sources can be treated as "reliable" or "correct". In all cases there are problems in the accuracy of the original estimates, number of different methods adopted, secrecy, and selectiveness and bias due to a wish to defend particular policies. Nevertheless the SIPRI data may be regarded as more reliable, in that SIPRI is more independent of the military establishment and more critical in evaluating the figures it publishes.

A number of other published sources can also be useful, although typically they contain little that is not in those cited above. *World Military and Social Expenditure*, edited by Ruth Sivard (obtainable from the Campaign Against the Arms Trade, 5 Caledonian Road, London N1 9DX) contrasts data on militarisation and the arms trade with social indicators of public expenditure and welfare. The UN publishes a *Disarmament Yearbook*. Various more or less academic journals such as the *Journal of Peace Research, Journal of Conflict Resolution, Current Research on Peace and Violence*, and *Bulletin of the Atomic Scientists* carry research reports that sometimes contain original data. Peace movement publications such as *Sanity* and *Peace News*, and sources such as *State Research Bulletin* and *New Statesman* often expose data that would otherwise be overlooked.

Coverage

There is plenty of data in the above sources on:
(i) Military expenditure totals. These are not however usually broken down by use (wages, equipment, etc.).
(ii) Weapon stocks: numbers of tanks, missiles, aircraft, etc. (IISS is particularly detailed here).
(iii) Troop numbers; though here there are particular problems with distinguishing military, paramilitary, security and civilian State employees.

There is some data, but much less, on the arms trade. As for arms production and profitability; the effects of nuclear weapons; and many other topics discussed in this pamphlet, these sources are typically rather silent.

Biases, distortion, etc.

Biases and distortion in.the available published data stem partly from the original source of the data, to which must be added any questionable assumptions, political bias, over-simplification, and so on, on the part of the publishers. As regards the latter factors, SIPRI data may be considered preferable.

The way the various factors combine in the case of specific data series is discussed in the main body of the pamphlet in the course of presenting the figures. We also discuss, on a more positive note, what conclusions *can* be drawn from the data.

Further reading

Critical assessments of the available military data may be found in Dan Smith, *The Defence of the Realm* (London, Croom Helm, 1980), especially Chapter 4; Dan Smith and Ron Smith, *The Economics of Militarism* (London, Pluto Press, forthcoming, 1982); and in U. Albrecht et al., *A short research guide on arms and armed forces* (London, Croom Helm, 1978).

FURTHER READING

In addition to the sources cited in the Appendix, the following provide information about nuclear weapons and nuclear war:

Cox J. *Overkill*. London: Penguin. 1981.
Goodwin P. *Nuclear War*. London: Ash and Grant. 1981.
Nield R. *How to make your mind up about the bomb*. London: Andre Deutsch. 1981.
Rogers P Dando M Van der Dungen P. *As lambs to the slaughter*. London: Arrow. 1981.
Rotblat J. *Nuclear radiation in warfare*. London: Taylor and Francis. 1981.
Smith D. *The defence of the realm in the 1980s*. London: Croom Helm. 1980.
ADIU Report. (ADIU, Mantell Building, University of Sussex, Brighton)

The following discuss disarmament action:

Myrdal A et al. (eds) *The dynamics of European nuclear disarmament*. Nottingham: Spokesman Books. 1981.
Ryle M. *The politics of nuclear disarmament*. London: Pluto Press. 1981.
Thompson EP. and Smith D. (eds.) *Protest and Survive*. London: Penguin. 1980.
END Bulletin (END, 227 Seven Sisters Rd London N4)
Peace News (Housemans Bookshop, 5 Caledonian Rd., London N1)
Sanity (CND, 11 Goodwin St., London N4)

GLOSSARY OF ABBREVIATIONS

ACDA   Arms Control and Disarmament Agency (Washington)
ADIU   Armaments and Disarmament Information Unit (Brighton)
ALCM   Air Launched Cruise Missile
CEP   Circular Error Probable
CIA   Central Intelligence Agency
CND   Campaign for Nuclear Disarmament
GLCM   Ground Launched Cruise Missile
ICBM   Intercontinental Ballistic Missile
IISS   International Institute of Strategic Studies (London)
MAD   Mutually Assured Destruction
MIRV   Multiple Independently Targeted Re-entry Vehicle
MOD   Ministry of Defence (London)
MX   Missile-Experimental
NATO   North Atlantic Treaty Organisation
R&D   Research and Development
SALT   Strategic Arms Limitations Talks
SLBM   Submarine Launched Ballistic Missile
SIPRI   Stockholm International Peace Research Institute
SRAM   Short Range Attack Missile
WP/WTO Warsaw Pact/Warsaw Treaty Organisation

The Radical Statistics Group was formed in 1975 by statisticians and research workers drawn together by a common concern about the political assumptions and implications of much of their work and of the actual and potential uses of statistical data and techniques. Membership of the group is open to all those working in or interested in statistics from a politically radical perspective.

Within Radical Statistics are groups with special interests in the political implications of applicatins of statistics in specific areas such as health, education, race relations and nuclear disarmament. The *Radical Statistics Newsletter* is circulated to all members of the group.

For further details please contact:
Radical Statistics,
c/o BSSRS,
9 Poland St.,
London W1V 3DG.

Previous Radical Statistics Group publications:

1. *Whose priorities? A critique of 'Priorities for health and personal services in England'*. 1976. 45p plus 20p p&p.
2. *In defence of the NHS. An attack on fee for service payments in medical care*. 1977. 50p plus 20p p&p.
3. *RAW(P) deals. A critique of 'Sharing resources for health in England'*. 1978. 25p plus 20p p&p.
4. *Social indicators: for individual well-being or social control? The case of OECD*. 1978. Out of print.
5. *The unofficial guide to official health statistics*. 1980. 2nd edition 1981. £1.00 (individuals, trades union branches, community groups); £2.00 (libraries and public institutions); £5.00 (private institutions and companies); plus 25p p&p.
6. *Britain's Black Population*. Produced by the Runnymede Trust and the Radical Statistics Race Group. Published by Heinemann Books. 1980. £4.95 paperback.
7. *A better start in life? Why perinatal statistics vary in different parts of the country* (audio tape). Produced by Radical Statistics Health Group and Local Radio Workshop. 1980. £1.50 plus 50p p&p. Available on cassette, with notes. £2.00 (individuals, community groups, trades union branches); £5.00 (others).

Forthcoming publications include:

9. *A guide to statistical methods for detecting health hazards at work*. To be published in 1982.
10. *Critical reading of educational research*. To be published in 1982.

Pamphlets 1, 2, 3 and 5 (also details of 9) can be obtained from the Radical Statistics Health Group; details of pamphlet 10 can be obtained from the Radical Statistics Education Group; (both groups at the address given above). Audiotape 7 can be obtained from Local Radio Workshop, 12 Praed Mews, London W2 1QY, (01) 402 7651.

Readers of our pamphlets may also find the following book of interest: *Demystifying Social Statistics*. Edited by John Irvine, Ian Miles, Jeff Evans. Published by Pluto Press. 1979. £4.95 paperback; £9.95 hardback.